THE C PROGRAMMING LANGUAGE

LANGUAGE

THE ULTIMATE BEGINNER'S GUIDE

BY

EASYPROGRAMMING PUBLISHER

THE C PROGRAMMING LANGUAGE
Copyright © 2016 by EasyProgramming Publisher

TABLE OF CONTENTS

INTRODUCTION

Thank you for buying this book: The C Programming Language –
The Ultimate Beginner's Guide. In this book, we are going to give
you an overview of the concepts that you have to understand before
you actually start programming in the C language. We will explain
to you the different elements that you ought to know about before
you go and delve into developing more complex programs for
different operating systems.

The C programming language has many benefits. However, it also
has numerous little aspects that can leave you perplexed. Not being
able to understand these aspects can definitely cause you problems
in the future.

In this book, we're going to talk about what those elements are. We
are also going to talk about what C is, where it came from, and all of
the fundamental concepts that you have to understand before you
actually start programming. In addition, we'll also teach you how to
setup and use the Code Blocks IDE, which will help you greatly
when programming in the C language.

We hope you enjoy this book.

CHAPTER 1: INTRODUCTION TO C PROGRAMMING LANGUAGE

Like anything new when you set out to do programming, you find yourself surrounded with strange and potentially weird terms, and fancied jargon. In this book, we'll review those terms as well as present an overview of the entire programming process. It is very likely that you're eager to get started with writing codes, and you may have already viewed a later chapter in this book. It is important to know a few key terms and programming concepts.

HISTORY OF C PROGRAMMING LANGUAGE

Back in 1972, a computer scientist at AT&T's Bell Laboratories started to develop some programs he needed for his own use. What Dennis Ritchie started developing then has evolved into the C programming language, which by now is widely used around the world.

He was trying to make computing as simple as possible. Dennis Ritchie realized that the then-current assembly language were much too complex. They attempted to reverse this trend by building a small, simple programming language on a minicomputer.

What Dennis Ritchie wanted to maintain was not only an efficient computer programming language in which to create programs, but also a computer programming language around which programming community could form—fellowship. They knew based from previous experiences that the real nature of joint computing as provided by time-shared, remote accessed systems is not just to enter computer code into a terminal, but to motivate post programming communication.

The C programming language is a general purpose and structured programming language. It is also called a procedural oriented programming language.

C is not specifically designed for specific application areas. However, it was well suited for business and scientific applications. It has various features like control structures, looping statements, and micros required for applications. The C language has the following features:

- Portability
- Flexibility
- Effectiveness and Efficiency
- Reliability
- Interactivity

WHAT IS PROGRAMMING?

Programming is where you create software. Software controls hardware, which is the physical part of an electronic device such as a computer, phone, tablet, gaming console, micro-controller or some other gizmo. Those instructions take the form of a programming language. For this book, that language is the C programming language, which was developed back in the early 1970s.

It is very old. In fact, over time the C programming language has been considered the Latin of programming languages. Unlike Latin, C is not dead. Lots of C programming still goes on despite of newer and fancier programming languages coming along. But like Latin, C is the foundation upon which many other programming languages are built. If you know C, you can more easily learn those other languages.

In a later chapter, we will talk about the programming language's syntax and other rules. But for now, know that the code you write is called a source code.

WHAT IS A SOURCE CODE?

A source code is a plain text file that contains the programming language, all formatted and pretty and written properly. In C, the file is saved with a .c filename extension. To create a source code, you use a text editor. Any text editor can do, although some editors offer helpful features like color coding, line numbers, syntax checking and other tools.

The source code is then compiled into object code. The program that creates the object code is called a compiler. The traditional name of the C language compiler is CC, which stands for C compiler. The compiler reads the source code file and generates an object code file.

Object code files have a .o filename extension, and they use the same filename as the original source code file. The next step is called Linking. It is often forgotten because modern compilers both compile and link, but linking is really a separate step.

The linker takes the object code file and combines it with C language libraries. The libraries are the workhorse of the language. They contain routines and functions that control whatever device you are programming. If all goes well, the end result is a program file. You can then test run the program to make sure that it works the way you want it to. And if not, you start the cycle all over again: edit, compile and link, or "build," and test run.

All of these tools—the editor, compiler, linker—all originated at the command prompt or terminal. You can still find them there too. Programmers do a lot of coding at the command prompt because it is quick. More common, however, is to use an IDE, or Integrated Development Environment.

WHAT IS AN IDE?

An IDE, or Integrated Development Environment, combines the tools for editing, compiling, linking, and running. It also adds tools for debugging, creating complex programs, graphical tools and other features.

Beneath it all, however, is the humble command line compiler and linker. The process is the same: edit, compile and link, run. You are going to do a lot of repeating and re-working before you get things right.

The good news is that all the tools you need to begin your programming journey are found free on the internet. The bad news being that you have to find the right tools and install them properly. This is not an issue for you here because in this book, we'll show you how it is done.

You will see how to find a good IDE, or Integrated Development Environment, a C language compiler, and get everything setup and configured. You will find a horde of IDEs on the Internet. Microsoft offers the Visual Studio as its IDE, and Apple has Xcode.

You are welcome to use those tools, especially if you are comfortable with them. But for this book, we have chosen the Code Blocks IDE. The great thing about Code Blocks is that it comes with everything you need. Unlike other IDEs, you don't have to hunt for this or that after the IDE is installed. You only have to download, configures, and you are ready to go. Obtain Code Blocks by visiting the developer's website: http://www.codeblocks.org.

Point your favorite browser—Chrome, Firefox, Internet Explorer—to that website. On that page, look for the download link. Remember, the page you see below may look different, as web pages do change from time to time.

Click on the download link. Choose to download the binary release. On the next page, click the link that represents your computer operating system: Windows, Linux, or Mac OSX. For Windows, look for the setup.exe file that includes the MinGW compiler. For example, on the screen below, it says "codeblocks-16.01mingw-setup.exe." The numbers may change, but that is the link you need.

For Linux, choose your 32-bit or 64-bit distro. Select a version of Code Blocks that is not testing or debuginfo. Try to match your specific Linux distro by choosing a link to download.

For the MAC, only one option is shown. Click the link to the right of your choice. We recommend that you use sourceforge.net as the download link. The download starts immediately. Wait until it is complete.

The next step is to find the downloaded file and install Code Blocks. Open the folder containing that file, which is usually the Downloads folder. You might also be able to access that folder from the web browser.

In Windows, double-click the file to open it and begin installation. Work through the installation wizard. Don't worry about any of the options. They are all okay. Eventually, Code Blocks will be installed with a shortcut icon on the desktop. Click the Yes button to start Code Blocks if you like, although it is not necessary to do so right away.

On the MAC and Linux, you need to unpack the archive you downloaded. Double-click the icon in a folder window to unpack the archive. On the MAC, you will end up with a Code Blocks app file, which is secretly a folder. We recommend moving that icon to the application's folder.

With Linux, double-click to open the archive. At that point, you will have to run the install program depending on how your Linux distro deals with whatever is in the archive. For example, if it is an RPM file, open it to begin package installation. After Code Blocks is installed, you need to get it configured. That topic is covered in another chapter.

RUNNING CODE BLOCKS

The main window will look like the illustration below:

This is known as the workspace. To the left, you will see the management panel. This lists the projects that you are working on in Code Blocks. The center is where you will find the editor where you will write the code. At the bottom, you will see a host of tabs. These can display messages or other useful information.

You should take a moment now to configure a few Code Blocks settings that will help you use the IDE in this book. First, choose settings editor. Ensure that there is a check-mark by the option "show line numbers." All the other options shown below should be set, which is the default.

Click the choose button in the font area to set the font. It is recommended that you use a mono-spaced font for clarity. Set your editor to a 12-point font so that it shows better on your screen. Click OK to close the general settings window.

Second, adjust the build messages text size. Choose Settings > Environment. Next, click the view icon. Set the message logs font size value to 10 or 12, which is better to see. Once you're done, click OK. Congratulations. Code Blocks is now configured for use together with this book.

You can quit Code Blocks now if you want. If you quit, you may be notified that the perspective has changed. Go ahead and save the perspective, and click on the little box so that you are not bothered with the message again.

14

Creating programs, or "Programming," usually involves typing the program's source code--instructions--using a programming language, and then compiles and links the source code together to create the program. The created program usually comes in the form of an .exe file if it is for the Windows operating system, or a .sh file if it is a UNIX based operating system like Linux or MAC.

You then test run the program to see if the program does what it's intended to do. In other words, run it to see if it is working. In the next chapter, we will show you a demonstration of how this process works in Code Blocks. We will talk about how to create and execute a sample computer program written in the C programming language. In addition, we will also teach you how to root out and fix bugs in your program using the IDE.

Once you've finished installing Code Blocks in your PC, start it up. You'll be presented with the Code Blocks start page. If by chance you're working on a computer that has Code Blocks already installed, and has been used to create programs previously, click on View > Start page on the Code Blocks menu to see the start page.

Majority of the work done on the Code Blocks IDE are project-oriented. Code Blocks C language projects can be a small and simple program, or a huge and complicated online computer game. Typically, Code Blocks projects are created by clicking the Create New Project link on the start page. Do note that this particular step is not required whenever you are viewing and working on C language project files that are taken from a different source other than your own computer.

But if you need to make a new C language project in the Code Blocks IDE, particularly the console programs/applications that we will be using in this book, then select the Console Application option when starting a brand new project.

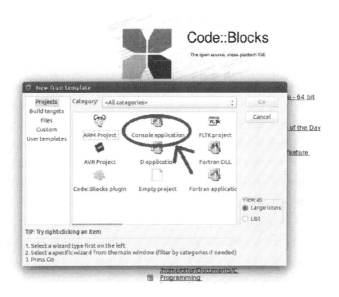

After choosing Console Application, select the C language option. Type in a name for the project and choose a folder where you will be saving the project file. On the Mac, ensure that the names don't have any spaces, or else the program can't be run from within Code Blocks. Choose "Release" only, and click Finish.

To open a pre-written source code file in Code Blocks, click the Open button on the toolbar. Browse to the folder containing the pre-written source code file. Choose the pre-written C file that you want to open and then click "Open." Then, you will see the source code that's written in that file in the Code Blocks editor window.

C code does not include line numbers, but the Code Block editor will show line numbers in the left most column. Line numbers are not only handy for reference in this book, but also great for tracking down errors. The source code itself appears on the right hand side of the line numbers. The Text is color-coded, which helps you recognize the different parts of C, as well as spot errors when things aren't colored correctly.

The next step after writing the source code is to compile and link. In Code Blocks, that step is combined into a single action called Build. To build your project, click the Build icon here:

The action takes place at the bottom of the screen in the Build log, and then Build messages tab. If there are errors in your source code, Code Blocks will display a small red box right beside the line number where the error resides. Click the Build log tab to review the specific messages related to the error.

The error messages will also indicate which line the error resides. If you spot an error in your code, rectify them and then click the Build button again. Once there are no more errors, save the file and re-build the project to make sure everything is okay.

Now, on the Macintosh, you may see a warning about option -s. That's a linker error and you can ignore it. Click the Run button to witness the program's brilliance. In Windows, the program runs in a command prompt window. On the Mac and Linux, a terminal window appears. In that window, you may also see any startup scripts you've written. Ignore that part of the output. Otherwise, what you see is the program's output.

Close the output window and return to Code Blocks. In Windows, press the Enter key. If the terminal window does not close in UNIX, just type "Exit" and then press the Enter key. It is recommended that you do this. Otherwise, the terminal windows will stack up. You're now ready to create your first project. If you shutdown Code Blocks, it will ask you whether or not you want to save the perspective. Go ahead and click Yes.

CHAPTER 2: STARING YOUR FIRST C PROJECT

The normal human language has two major parts: syntax and speech. Likewise, the C programming language also has its own syntax and speech. If a person who has no background in computer programming looks at a computer source code, it is likely that they won't be able to make heads or tails out of it. However, once they learn the syntax and the figures of speech of the programming language, it will all begin to make sense.

In this book, we will introduce you to syntax and figures of speech of the C programming language. We will teach you how it is structured, what the main function actually does, and also familiarize yourself with its various functions, keywords, values, variables, and operators.

In the Code Blocks IDE, go ahead and click the "New" button, and then click "Empty file." At this point, you're now going to type a C programming language code in the editor window pane of the Code Blocks IDE. Don't be afraid. You're going to type only one line.

Go ahead and type the word "main," followed by a pair of parenthesis and a space, and then lastly, followed by a pair of curly braces or brackets. Once you finish typing that in, press Enter on the keyboard. Your Code Blocks editor should now look like this:

```
1        main() {}
2
```

Now, save the source code file by clicking the Save button. If you need to, choose the specific folder where you want to save your C programming language source code files. Type the filename "dummy.c" for the file. The source code file is now created and saved. Next, click the Build button.

The code does compile. What you see is the absolute minimum C program known as "The dummy." All C source code must have the main function. This is where the program execution starts. The contents of the main function are enclosed in curly brackets.

In our dummy source code, everything is empty, which is okay. However, you might see a compiler warning, which isn't critical. A program was created. Click the Run button to run the dummy program. You will notice that there is no output. That is to be expected because the program code does nothing.

Like any language, the C programming language has several parts:

- Keywords
- Functions
- Operators
- Values and Variables
- Structure

KEYWORDS

The keywords are the language part of the C language. They accomplish very basic tasks. The good news is that, unlike English which has tens of thousands of words, there are only 44 words in the C language. In practice, you may only use about half of these keywords.

_Alignas	break	float	signed
_Alignof	case	for	sizeof
_Atomic	char	goto	static
_Bool	const	if	struct
_Complex	continue	inline	switch
_Generic	default	int	typedef
_Imaginary	do	long	union
_Noreturn	double	register	unsigned
_Static_assert	else	restrict	void
_Thread_local	enum	return	volatile
auto	extern	short	WHILE

FUNCTIONS

The real workhorses of the C language are functions. What the keywords do is really basic. To do more in C, you rely upon a function. The functions are held in libraries. The linker's job is to combine the library with your program's object code; knitting the two together to make a program.

To use a function in a program, you must incorporate a header file, which defines the function. You will see how that's done in the later chapters.

OPERATORS

Operators are symbols used to manipulate data in the program. These include the traditional math operators, as well as a host of other special symbols.

- Mathematical: +-/*%++--
- Comparison: == != > <
- Assignment: = += -+ *= /=
- Logical: && || !
- Bitwise: & | ^ << >>
- Unary + - ~ ! *

Values and Variables

Values and variables are similar. Values include characters and numeric values. The numeric values are divided between integers or whole numbers, and floating-point values which contain a decimal part or fraction. All of them can be very, very large values, or very, very small values.

A variable, on the other hand, is a container for a value. Its contents can change or vary, which is why they are called variables. The values that go into the variables are the same types of values you use directly in a program.

STRUCTURE

Every piece of the C programming language must be utilized in a particular order or manner. This is what's called as the C programming language structure. To assist in controlling the program flow, the C programming language makes use of preprocessor directives. The first function that is run in every C language program is the main function. The main function is a major requirement in every C language program. Without it, the program will not compile, much less run.

Curly braces/brackets are utilized to enclose the contents of the function. What amounts to sentences in the C programming language area are what we call "Statements". Statements include but are not limited to C language functions, keywords, logical comparisons, math, and so on.

Finally, we have the "comments." Comments are notes for other programmers, or yourself, who will be looking at the source code. Comments serve as general information or reminders and are not compiled as part of the source code by the compiler. Now since you now have a little background, let us put it to use by completing the dummy C language program that we wrote previously.

Return to the dummy.c program's source code in the IDE's editor. The main function is defined as an integer function. That means it returns an integer value to the operating system. Therefore, some editing is necessary. In your editor, type the C language keyword "int" before the word "main" and ensure that a space separates both like so:

```
1       int main() {}
2
```

Next, clean up the curly brackets, which most veteran programmers prefer to put each on a line by itself.

```
1        int main()
2        {
3        }
```

Now, let's add a statement to the main function. Note how the editor automatically indents the line. That's the traditional way C code is formatted. Next, type the word "return" and a number. Go ahead and pick any number, although it must be an integer. In our example, we'll type the number 3.

```
1        int main()
2        {
3                return(3);
4        }
5
```

You can type the number in parenthesis, as what we've done in the example shown above, or you can just specify the value. If so, you need to put a space between return and the value like so:

```
1        int main()
2        {
3                return 3;
4        }
5
```

Don't forget to type a semi-colon to end the statement. Save the file and then click Build. As long as your code looks like the example shown above, no errors or warnings will appear. Go ahead and click Run.

On the Mac or Linux, you may see no output other than the build log, and it says the program terminated with status zero. On the PC, the terminal window shows you the return value as 3, which is the integer value specified in the return statement.

To add output to the dummy program, you need to use an output function. C language keywords don't output anything. They are just basic vocabulary, words like return and int. As an example of an output function, you can use *puts*, which sends text to the standard output device. In this case, it is the terminal window.

Program code in the C language is read top-down because the return statement ends the main function. Add the *puts* function at line 3 of our dummy program by inserting a new line into the editor.

In the puts function's parenthesis, you place a string of text, which consist of characters snuggled between double quotes. Go ahead and type any string of text that you want.

```
1       int main()
2       {
3               puts("I am the King of the C programming world");
4               return 3;
5       }
6
```

Again, don't forget to put a semi-colon at the end of the *puts* function's line. Save the source code and then click Build. At this point, you may or may not see a warning. Even if you don't, you need to know that the *puts* function requires a definition before it can be used. Otherwise, the compiler becomes confused.

The definition is held in the standard I/O header file. You must include that header file in your source code by using the include preprocessor directive. To do that, first you must insert a line at the top of the source code. Then, type "#," the word "include", a left angled bracket, the word "stdio.h," and a right angled bracket. Put another line for readability. Your code should now look like the one below:

```
1       #include <stdio.h>
2
3       int main()
4         {
5               puts("I am the King of the C Programming
world");
6               return 3;
7         }
8
```

This preprocessor directive includes the definition for the *puts* function. Save the file, but this time, click the Build and Run button near the top right of the editor, which is two steps in one. If you type everything correctly, there will be no warnings or errors. On the output terminal window, you'll see the string that you specified for the puts function and the return value 3.

CHAPTER 3: THE OLD I/O

The best way to get started on your programming journey is to write some simple programs that are easy to understand and change. To handle that task, it helps to know the basics of input and output, or I/O.

In this chapter, we introduce you to the concept of I/O, and how that plays into programming. You will get to explore some basic I/O functions, and use one of those functions to create tiny programs that output interesting text.

A program has to do something. That something involves taking input and generating output. This is how a typical C program works: it's a machine that does something to input, and then generates output.

If the program does not do anything, then it is basically plumbing; what comes in, goes out. The C library offers a host of output functions. Of the lot, these three are the most popular. They are:

- printf()
- putchar()
- puts()

PUTS FUNCTION

Each function is designed to send one or more characters to the standard output device, which is the screen or terminal window. The puts function puts, or sends a string of text to standard output. "Puts" is put string, and a string is a collection of characters enclosed in double quotes. This function is defined in the STDIO.IO header file, which is included at line one of your dummy program.

In the source code below, we've specified the puts function, but omitted the string. Your job is to type this source code in your editor, and supply the string.

```
1       #include <stdio.h>
2
3       int main()
4       {
5               puts();
6
7               return(0);
8       }
9
10
```

Click inside side the parenthesis and type the string argument for the "puts" function. Type a double quote. The editor automatically supplies the closing quote. Type the text of your choice. If the editor does not supply the closing quote, you must type it. Otherwise, the compiler will not see the end of the string, and an ugly error will be generated.

```
1       #include <stdio.h>
2
3       int main()
4         {
5               puts("This is just an example");
6
7               return(0);
8         }
9
10
```

You can also type the quote even if it is supplied. The Code Block editor is smart enough not to double up. The string that you type will be highlighted in blue. Click save, build, and run. As you can see in the output, it displays the string exactly as you typed.

Adding multiple stdio.h header files when using multiple puts functions in your source code is not required. One is all you need. Also, you can type a single quote within a pair of double quotes. That's not a problem. Again, remember to end the statement with a semi-colon.

Next, let's try adding comments to the previous source code example. As what we've mentioned previously, comments are text that doesn't compile. Instead, it is intended for the programmer as a reminder, or just general information.

First, insert a new line at the top of your source code file. Type a slash "/", and then an asterisk "*" symbol. Traditional C comments start with a slash-asterisk character combination, and end with the asterisk and slash characters.

```
1     /*
2     #include <stdio.h>
3
4     int main()
5     {
6             puts("Hello Mr. Programmer");
7             puts("I'm thrilled to meet you");
8
9             return(0);
10    }
11
```

At this point, the editor highlights all the text in the code, which is not effectively one long comment because no ending comment characters have been written in our sample code above. Next, type your name and the date like so:

```
1     /* Charles Xavier October 10, 2016 */
2     #include <stdio.h>
3
```

```
4        int main()
5        {
6                puts("Hello Mr. Programmer");
7                puts("I'm thrilled to meet you");
8
9                return(0);
10       }
11
```

After typing your name and date, type an asterisk and a slash to end the comment. As we've mentioned earlier, comments aren't compiled, and you can prove it. Go ahead and save the changes to the source code, click Build and Run, and you will see that the output only displays the string arguments you specified for the puts functions.

A second type of comment uses two slash symbols "//" at the start of the line. You can use this comment to disable a statement in the code, which happens a lot when you are hunting down bugs or trying to fix something. Let's try it out in line 6 of our previous example:

```
1        /* Charles Xavier October 10, 2016 */
2        #include <stdio.h>
3
4        int main()
5        {
6        //      puts("Hello Mr. Programmer");
7                puts("I'm thrilled to meet you");
```

```
8
9                    return(0);
10      }
11
```

Save the code, and then click Build and Run. See how the output doesn't appear? That's because the compiler treated it like a comment. If you'd like to restore the line, remove the // comment, then save, and then build and run your code again. Before ending this section, we would like you to view the files created when you build a program in C.

Open the folder where you saved your C language source code files. For each source code file, you find an object code file. It has the same name as the source code file, but with a .o filename extension. That's the file created by the compiler. The object code file contains both the compiled source code, as well as information from the header file.

The linker takes that object code file and mixes in the C library file. The result is a program file, which also has the same name as the source code file. In Windows, you may see the filename extension .exe, which means executable. In other operating systems, no extension is necessary.

The program file might also be given the name a.exe or a.out. That's the linker's default name. Although in Code Blocks, the program name is the same as the source code file's name.

PRINTF FUNCTION

If there's one favorite C programming language function programmers love to use, it is the *printf* function. The *printf* function is the first function every novice programmer learns because it is part of the traditional "Hello World" computer program. However, the *printf* function can do more than just display or output text in the screen. In this section, we will talk about the *printf* function.

As most of you already know, the *printf* function is one of the C programming language's many text output functions. However, it is much more powerful than the *puts* function. Also, we will talk about how to use various escape sequences in your code. Sending an array of characters--strings--to standard output is the *printf* function's most basic form. In other words, it shows the user/programmer a bunch of text on the computer screen.

Just like the *puts* function, the *printf* function is defined within the header file *stdio.h*. If you look at the code below, you'll see that the *printf* function is utilized twice, specifically at lines 5 and 6:

```
1       #include <stdio.h>
2
3       int main()
4       {
5               printf("This the way the world ends");
6               printf("Not with a bang but a whimper");
7
8               return(0);
```

```
9      }
10
11
```

In this mode, printf works a lot like the puts function. The argument for printf is a single string held between the function's parentheses. The string is enclosed in double quotes. If you're following along, save and run this code. As you can see, the program doesn't air the output as it should be. This is because unlike the puts function, the printf function does not add a new line character at the end of the string.

Yes, even though two statements are used on two lines of code, the output is one long string. To add the new line, which is like pressing the Enter key at the end of a line, you must specify an escape character.

Edit line 5 of our previous code above to insert a backslash and a small letter 'n' before the ending double quote. In some editors, the backslash 'n' appears in a different color, showing that it is special. Save your changes and then build and run the code. Now, you will see two lines of output.

```
1      #include <stdio.h>
2
3      int main()
4      {
5          printf("This the way the world ends\n");
6          printf("Not with a bang but a whimper");
```

```
7
8                       return(0);
9       }
10
11
```

ESCAPE CHARACTERS

There are some characters you just can't put into a string. To sneak around this limitation, you use Escape characters. In the C language, a string is a bunch of characters held between two double quotes. Everything between the double quotes counts. But sometimes you can't type a character such as the Enter key.

For example, if you wanted to put the Enter key press between two words in a string and create a new line of text, the result would be two lines in the editor, not on the output. The solution is to use the '\n' character in the string. It is an Escape character, which means it starts with a backslash, and then followed by the letter 'n' for newline. Take a look at the example below:

"Behold! \n I am a string of text."

Together, the '\n' is interpreted as one character—a new line—and it is generated when the string is output. The C language uses about a dozen of Escape characters also known as escape sequences. The most common are:

- \n – new line, to start a new line of text
- \t – tab, to hop over so many spaces

- \' - escaped single quote
- \" - escaped double quote
- \\ - display backspace characters

Now, let's say that you want to print a string in two lines, and indicates your name in double quotes. How would you do it? How would you ensure that the double quotes that will be enclosing your name would be displayed as a string and not as part of the source code? Well, here's how:

```
1       #include <stdio.h>
2
3       int main()
4       {
5               printf("Hello!\nMy name is \"Hector.\"");
6
7               return(0);
8       }

10
```

As you can see from our sample code above, we've inserted a '\n' character immediately after "Hello!" so as to put the succeeding strings on a new line, and then enclose the name 'Hector' between two escaped double quotes, so that the double quotes will be treated as a string.

You can also choose to remove the escaped double quotes and replace them with single quotes. Why? Because single quotes in a string do not need to be escaped. Many programmers find this method easier to use.

On the other hand, a value is typically numeric, although it doesn't have to be. In your code, you can specify values such as three, five, or even 100,000,000. You can make use of the *printf* function to output those values providing you know about something called a placeholder. In the next section, we'll continue exploring the *printf* function. We'll show you how placeholders can be used to display values, not only number, but strings and individual characters as well.

To view values in action, you can use the *printf* function. But you have to take that function up a notch. Take a look at your sample code below:

```
1       #include <stdio.h>
2
3       int main()
4       {
5               printf("Here is a value: 27\n");
6
7               return(0);
8       }
9
10
```

The *printf* function in line 5 of our sample code above generates an output that would have you believe that the number 27 was a value, but it is not. It is part of a string—just the characters 2 and 7. To specify a value, you need to do two things. First, you must place a value into the code—in this case the number 27. Second, you must direct the *printf* function to display that value.

Edit line five to replace the characters 2 and 7 with '%d.' In some editors, you may see the %d highlighted. That is because it is a special symbol for the *printf* function. It is a placeholder. In this case, it is a placeholder for an integer value—a whole number. Place a comma after the string and add a second argument to the *printf* function: the value 27.

Note how a value is shown in its own color in the Code Blocks editor. The printf function now has two arguments. The first is called the formatting string. It contains one placeholder, which is %d. Matching that placeholder is the second argument: the integer value 27. Your code should now look like this:

```
1       #include <stdio.h>
2
3       int main()
4       {
5               printf("Here is a value: %d\n", 27);
6
7               return(0);
8       }
9
10
```

Now save, build and run the code. In the output, 27 represent the value 27. Its output is text, of course. But inside the program, it is a number and not text. Now, copy line five of our sample code in line 6 and then change the number to 29. Save, build and run your code.

```
1       #include <stdio.h>
2
3       int main()
4       {
5               printf("Here is a value: %d\n", 27);
6               printf("Here is a value: %d\n", 29);
7
8               return(0);
9       }
10
11
```

As you can see, two lines are output. The same placeholder is used in both *printf* functions. However, because a different value is specified, the new value is output for the second statement. The %d placeholder is just that—it holds the place of another argument. In fact, you can specify multiple placeholders providing that you have arguments to match, just like in line 7 of the code below:

```
1       #include <stdio.h>
2
3       int main()
4       {
5               printf("Here is a value: %d\n", 27);
```

```
6            printf("Here is a value: %d\n", 29);
7            printf("Here are the values %d, %d, and
%d\n", 51,52,53);
7
8            return(0);
9       }
```

You can even do math in a printf function. Although, it is the C language that does the math, not the printf function. Take a look at the code below:

```
1       #include <stdio.h>
2
3       int main()
4       {
5               printf("Everyone knows that 2+2=%d\n", 4);
6
7               return(0);
8       }
9
10
```

Here you see an immediate value specified in the printf statement. However, math isn't always going to be that simple. Replace the four with the equation two plus two like so:

```
1       #include <stdio.h>
2
3       int main()
```

```
4        {
5                printf("Everyone knows that 2+2=%d\n",
2+2);
6
7                return(0);
8        }
9
10
```

Now save, build and run. In this instance, the program makes the calculation for you. It adds two and two, and the result is fetched from the %d placeholder in the *printf* statement. Now, replace the equation in line five with this: 278*956. On the computer, the asterisk is used as the multiplication operator. We'll officially discuss that, as well as other math concepts in the later chapters.

Moving forward, change the format string as well, replacing two plus two with 278 x 956. Now save, build and run. Apparently the result is 265,768.

```
1        #include <stdio.h>
2
3        int main()
4        {
5                printf("Everyone knows that 278 x
956=%d\n", 278*956);
6
7                return(0);
8        }
9
10
```

The *printf* statement employs a swath of placeholders, each for a specific type of value. Below is a partial list showing some of the more common placeholders:

- %d   Integer (whole number) values
- %s   Strings
- %f   Floating-point values or fractions
- %c   Single characters
- %%   The percent sign

It helps to know about the different types of values in the C language before you can use each of these, as well as understand the whole lot of them that are not shown. Also, the placeholders have options that we'll get into in the later chapters.

The %s placeholder is used to display strings. It may look a little odd. However it does come in handy. Take a look at the code below:

```
1       #include <stdio.h>
2
3       int main()
4       {
5               printf("You are a %s\n", "programmer");
6
7               return(0);
8       }
9
10
```

In this code, the %s placeholder represents the string "programmer," which is the second argument of the *printf* function. If you are following along, build and run the code above. Now, modify line five of the code above to add another placeholder and another argument to the *printf* function. Place %c before %s and squeeze a space between the two like so:

```
1       #include <stdio.h>
2
3       int main()
4       {
5               printf("You are a %s\n", "programmer");
6
7               return(0);
8       }
9
10
```

Now you have to add an argument for the %c. After the comma, type a single quote, followed by a big C, another singe quote, and then a comma. Many editors will assign the single character value to its own color, as you will see when you type the code in Code Blocks.

```
1       #include <stdio.h>
2
3       int main()
4       {
5               printf("You are a %c %s\n", 'C',
"programmer");
```

```
6
7              return(0);
8      }
9
10
```

In the C language, single characters are specified by single quotes. If you use double quotes, you create a one character string. That's not what you need to match the %c placeholder. Save your code, build, and run. As you can see from the output, it'll output the string "You are a C programmer."

One final thing, because the percent character is used as a placeholder, you must specify two of them when you use a percent symbol in the *printf* statement's formatting string. Take a look at the code below:

```
1      #include <stdio.h>
2
3      int main()
4      {
5              printf("I got %d% on my C exam!\n", 98);
6
7              return(0);
8      }
9
10
```

Read the *printf* statement in the code above. The %d placeholder should match up with the second argument, which is 98. It is followed by a percent sign, which indicates actual percentage, not a placeholder. Build and run this code. Now, if you don't see any warnings, that's okay. The output is still going to look weird. In some compilers, you will see warnings that indicate trouble.

The compiler believes that a second placeholder is desired. It does not understand the placeholder as presented. Plus, it can't find a matching argument. If you don't see the warning, try to run the code and see what happens.

The solution is to edit line five and stick in another percent sign. It looks odd, and it is cryptic. It is the cryptic side of the C language, in fact, that enthralls so many of the nerds. However, it is going to work.

```
1       #include <stdio.h>
2
3       int main()
4       {
5               printf("I got %d%% on my C exam!\n", 98);
6
7               return(0);
8       }
9
10
```

Save the changes, build and run. Now, the output looks more sensible.

CHAPTER 4: THE C LANGUAGE VARIABLES

Programs work fine with immediate values. But oftentimes, you don't know what the value is. Say the value comes from input, the user types it. It is read from a file or the Internet. To store such values, you need a specific cubby-hole or container. In programming, that container is known as a variable. In this chapter, we introduce you to the concept of the variable. It is a container into which you can store values—values that are unknown or values that can change.

You'll see how to declare a variable in the C language, and how a variable is used in the code. A variable is a container for a value. Because C deals with different types of values, a variable must be declared as a specific type. It is given a name—a name that's used in the code.

In C, the variable type matches the variable's content—the type of value being stored. Integer variables can hold only integer values or whole numbers. Float variables hold floating-point values, which are very large numbers, very small numbers, or numbers with a fractional part.

Character variables hold single values such as the letter 'x.' The C language lacks a string variable type. Instead, a character array is used. We'll discuss how that works in a later chapter.

The *int, float,* and *char* are all C language keywords. Additional keywords are also used to declare variables. These include double, long, short, signed, and unsigned. These are all C language keywords that are used to declare different types of variables. Take a look at the code below:

```
1        #include <stdio.h>

2

3        int main()

4        {

5                int age;

6

7                age = 30;

8                printf("The C language is over %d years
old!\n", age);

9

10               return(0);

11       }

12
```

This code declares an integer variable at line five. First comes the keyword *int*, which is used to declare an integer variable. Next come the variable name: age. As this is a statement, it ends with a semi-colon. Variable names can include numbers, letters, and some symbols. They must begin with a letter, or an underline. The name must be unique, with no two variables having the same name, nor should variables have the same name as functions or C language keywords.

At line seven, the variable *age* is assigned the value 30. In C, values or equations go on the right side of the assignment operator, the equal sign. The value or results of the equation is then assigned to the variable on the left. Because 30 is an integer value, it fits nicely into the integer variable *age*.

The statement at line nine displays the variable's value by using the *printf* function. The %d placeholder is used, and the variable *age* is specified as the second argument. Now go ahead and build and run the code. The whole idea behind the variable is that its value can change. Edit the source code so that the value of the *age* variable is changed to 34. Make this modification at line seven.

```
1       #include <stdio.h>
2
3       int main()
4       {
5               int age;
6
7               age = 34;
8               printf("The C language is over %d years
old!\n", age);
9
10              return(0);
11      }
12
```

Save the modified code, then build and run it. As you will see, the program's output reflects the new value.

Now, assign a new value to the variable in the code by adding two lines after line eight. First, assign the value 50 to the age variable:

```
1       #include <stdio.h>
2
3       int main()
4       {
5               int age;
6
7               age = 34;
8               printf("The C language is over %d years
old!\n", age);
9               age = 50;
10
11
12
13              return(0);
14      }
15
```

Second, type another printf function:

```
1       #include <stdio.h>
2
3       int main()
4       {
5               int age;
6
7               age = 34;
8               printf("The C language is over %d years
old!\n", age);
9               age = 50;
```

```
10              printf("The programmer is over %d years
old\n", age);
11
12              return(0);
13      }
14
```

Save the above changes, then build and run the code. See how the *age* variable is used twice, but hold two different integer values. On your own, you can change this code once more. This time you can assign your own age to the age variable and simply add a printf statement to say how old you are.

Math can also be performed using variables. Take a look at the code below:

```
1       #include <stdio.h>
2
3       int main()
4       {
5               int age;
6
7               age = 32;
8               printf("%s is %d years old!\n", "James", age);
9               printf("That's %d months!\n", age*12);
10
11              return(0);
12      }
13
```

In line seven, the value 32 is assigned to the variable integer *age*. Edit the value to reflect your own age in years. The *printf* function in line eight uses two statements: a string and an integer variable. The string is an immediate value. Change the name "James" to your own name, unless your name is also James.

You don't need to guess how many months you have because that value is calculated as the argument in the *printf* function at line nine. Save the code, build and run. Of course, the month's value displayed is an approximation, unless today is your birthday. In that case, Happy Birthday!

The *int* is really one variable type. Another common type is the char or character variable. Take a look at the code below:

```
1       #include <stdio.h>
2
3       int main()
4       {
5               char x, y, z;
6
7               x = 'A';
8               y = 'B';
9               z = 'C';
10
11              printf("It's as easy as %c%c%c\n", x,y,z);
12
13              return(0);
14      }
15
```

Here, three character variables are declared: *x*, *y*, and *z*. You can declare multiple variables of the same type on a single line, as long as each variable name is separated by a comma. Lines 7-9 assign the variables characters—single quotes are used. Then the values are displayed by the *printf* function at line 11. Save, build, and run the code.

Just as you can change integer variables, you can also change character variables. You can even do math. Edit line eight to read:

```
1       #include <stdio.h>
2
3       int main()
4         {
5               char x, y, z;
6
7               x = 'A';
8               y = x+1;
9               z = 'C';
10
11              printf("It's as easy as %c%c%c\n", x,y,z);
12
13              return(0);
14        }
15
```

Then, edit line nine to read:

```
1       #include <stdio.h>

2

3       int main()

4       {

5               char x, y, z;

6

7               x = 'A';

8               y = x+1;

9               z = y+1;

10

11              printf("It's as easy as %c%c%c\n", x,y,z);

12

13              return(0);

14      }

15
```

Save, build and run the code. The output is the same. Instead of assigning immediate values to variables *y* and *z*, you did a little character math. Adding 1 to the value of character A gives you a B, and adding 1 to the value of B gives you a C.

The final variable type that we would like to introduce is the float. It holds very large values, very small values, or any values with a fractional part. Take a look at the code below:

```
1       #include <stdio.h>

2

3       int main()

4       {
```

```
5                float pi;

6

7                pi = 22.00 / 7.0;

8                printf("The ancients calculated PI as %f.\n",

pi);

9

10               return(0);

11       }

12

13
```

The float variable *pi* is declared at line five. At line seven, a calculation is made and the result is assigned to the variable *pi*. The calculation uses floating point values. By adding a .00 to 22 and 7, the compiler assumes that you need floating point values and treats them as such. Otherwise, integers would be used, and the result would be wrong.

When you use a floating point whole number, remember to add the .00. Line eight sends the result to standard output. The %f placeholder is used to represent floating point values in a *printf* statement. Build and run the code.

The value generated for pi is accurate down to the hundreds place, which is okay for quite a few things in antiquity, but not acceptable for modern calculations.

CHAPTER 5: CHARACTER I/O FUNCTIONS IN C

Programs are both known for input and output. Output goes to the standard output device, which is usually the screen or terminal window. Input comes from the standard input device, which is normally the keyboard. In this chapter, we'll explore input and output concepts in C. These involve character I/O, which is the reading of single characters, as well as the output of a single character. We'll also touch upon the concept of stream input and output.

The two most common C language character I/O functions are *getchar()* and *putchar()*. *Getchar()* fetches the standard input. *Putchar()* sends a character to standard output. Both of these functions require the inclusion of the stdio.h header file for their prototypes and such.

Although they are character functions, they work with integer values. Yes, that's weird, but so are many things in the C language. In fact, you may find yourself frequently using *char* variables with these functions. When you do, the compiler may gently warn you about the mistake. Finally, these functions are stream oriented, which is something we'll discuss in the later chapters.

Take a look at the code below:

```
1       #include <stdio.h>
2
```

```
3       int main();
4       {
5               int c;
6
7               printf("Type a letter: ");
8               c = getchar();
9               printf("You typed '%c'.\n", c);
10
11              return(0);
12      }
13
```

Integer variable C is declared at line 5. It is used with the *getchar()* function at line eight, storing a single character from the input stream. In this example, that would be a character typed at the keyboard. The character is displayed at line nine. The int variable C is used, but the character placeholder %c is specified. This ensures that the character is displayed, not its code value. Build and run the code.

Note that the prompt in the output keeps the cursor at the same line, and we've added a space to make it more readable. Type a letter, such as a big letter 'Z,' and press the Enter key. As you can see in the output, it will immediately specify the letter that you typed.

Now, modify the code so that the *putchar()* function outputs the character you typed. To do that, you need to split the *printf* function in two, like so:

```
1       #include <stdio.h>
2
3       int main();
4       {
5               int c;
6
7               printf("Type a letter: ");
8               c = getchar();
9               printf("You typed '");
10              putchar(c);
11              printf("'.\n");
12
13              return(0);
14      }
15
```

Edit it to where it says, "You typed" and notice how we kept that single quote after that string. Close the string in parenthesis and end the statement with a semi-colon. Then add *putchar()* on line ten, and then display the rest of the string by using *printf*. The argument C is no longer needed. Instead, it appears in line ten with the *putchar()* function where it is output directly. Save, build and run the source code file.

The solution provides for the putchar() function to generate output. But it also makes the code longer and less readable. That is actually okay in C, and you'll discover that the output is unchanged. Save, build and run the code.

You can also use the putchar() function with immediate values. At this point in the code, the statement at line 11 really just outputs three characters: the single quote, period, and the new line. We could change line 11 to read:

```
1       #include <stdio.h>
2
3       int main();
4       {
5               int c;
6
7               printf("Type a letter: ");
8               c = getchar();
9               printf("You typed '");
10              putchar(c);
11              putchar('\'')
12              printf("'.\n");
13
14              return(0);
15      }
16
```

At line 11, type a single quote, a backslash, a single quote, and then another single quote. That looks odd, but you have to escape the single quote character. Otherwise, the compiler becomes confused. A second *putchar()* function would display the period. The final *putchar()* function would display the escape sequence, which is specified in the original *printf* function as a new line.

```
1       #include <stdio.h>
2
3       int main();
4       {
5               int c;
6
7               printf("Type a letter: ");
8               c = getchar();
9               printf("You typed '");
10              putchar(c);
11              putchar('\"')
12              putchar('.')
13              putchar('\n');
14
15              return(0);
16      }
17
```

We have three *putchar()* functions instead of a single *printf* function that displays a three character string. Save the changes, build and run. As you will see, the output is the same. Now take a look at the code below:

```
1       #include <stdio.h>
2
3       int main()
4       {
5               int a, b;
6
```

```
7               printf("Type two letters: ");
8               a = getchar();
9               b = getchar();
10              printf("You typed '");
11              putchar(a);
12              printf("' and '");
13              putchar(b);
14              printf("'.\n");
15
16              return(0);
17      }
18
```

Here, two *getchar()* functions fetch two characters. These characters are then displayed using a series of *printf* and *putchar()* functions. Build and run the code. Type any two letters that you like. The two characters you type are stored in variables *a* and *b*, and the displayed.

Note that the *getchar()* function do not pause and wait for input. They simply look for all input coming from the standard input device like a stream of characters flowing out of a hose. To demonstrate this phenomenon, run the previous code again. But this time, just type the letter 'z' and press the Enter key.

The weird output that you will see is the code displaying the new-line character, which was stored in variable *b*. Run the code again. But this time, type several letters and then press the Enter key. For the sake of an example, let's say you typed the letters *a*, *b*, *c*, *d*, and *e* respectively.

The entire stream of characters—a through e—that you will see on your screen are fed into the program via the standard input. The *getchar()* function read only the first two. But our input persisted until we pressed the Enter key. The stream input could also be demonstrated by examining the code below:

```
1       #include <stdio.h>
2
3       int main()
4       {
5               int a, b, c;
6
7               printf("Type three letters: ");
8               a = getchar();
9               putchar(a);
10              b = getchar();
11              putchar(b);
12              c = getchar();
13              putchar(c);
14
15              return(0);
16      }
17
```

Here, it looks like one character is fetched by *getchar()* and then immediately gets displayed by *putchar()*. That's logical because C programs run top down, and they do. That's exactly what happens in this program, but it's not what you see when the code runs. Build and run the code. Type a, b, c, or any other three letters and press the Enter key.

The output happens all at once because of the stream. The characters you typed are actually sent to output as you type them, which is how the code runs. However, stream output is buffered. That means that the computer waits until the buffer is full or flushed before sending out the characters. In this case, the buffer is flushed once the program is finished. We'll explore stream input and output further in the later chapters. But for now, remember that the standard C I\O library functions are stream oriented.

THE STRING

A character is a single letter or symbol. Put two characters together and you have a string. But strings are funky things in the C programming language. They are not a variable type, just a clutch or array of characters all marching together in a line.

In this section, we'll introduce you to the string. You'll see how strings are created in C—how they can be filled by using string input functions. You'll also meet the scanf() function, which is used to pull in all sorts of input. Take a look at the code below:

```
1       #include <stdio.h>
2
3       int main()
4       {
5               char password[] = "spatula";
6
```

```
7              printf("The password is \"%s\"\n",
password);
8
9              return(0);
10      }
11
12
```

Line 5 probably looks a little odd to you. It is a variable declaration. A char variable named password is created, then the string "spatula" is assigned to the password variable. This is known as an immediate assignment, which is possible with other variables as well. When declaring a string, immediate assignments are an absolute necessity.

By the way, line 5 of the code is an array declaration, which is a topic for a later chapter. The square brackets indicate that more than one char variable is present. How many? The compiler figures that out based on the size of the string. Otherwise, the value would appear between the brackets.

In line 7, a printf function displays the string's value. The %s placeholder is used—it is difficult to see because of the escaped double quotes and the new line. Build and run this code. The output properly shows the contents of the string. Change the word "spatula" in your editor to the words, "fuzzy wuzzy".

```
1       #include <stdio.h>
2
3       int main()
```

```
4       {
5                   char password[] = "fuzzy wuzzy";
6
7                   printf("The password is \"%s\"\n",
password);
8
9                   return(0);
10      }
11
12
```

Make sure to put a space between each word, as spaces are valid characters on some systems. Save the changes and then build and run the code to see the changes displayed.

Remember that some characters must be escaped in a string. These include double quotes, new line, tab, and so on.

THE SCANF() FUNCTION

To fetch a string from standard input, use the *scanf()* function. As an input function, *scanf()* is declared in the stdio.h header file, which you must include in your code, lest the compiler becomes confused.

Scanf() uses *printf()*'s placeholder to read a specific value into a variable, and that variable is often prefixed with the ampersand symbol. Here's the format for the *scanf()* function:

   scanf("forat", &variable);

It includes two arguments: a formatted string and a variable. The formatted string directs *scanf()* to look for a specific type of value. To accomplish this, you specify the same placeholder used with the *printf* function inside the formatting string. %d for an integer, %c for a character, and so on. The formatting string is almost always composed of these placeholders and nothing else.

To assign a value, specify the variable that's already been declared in the code. The variable type must match the placeholder. You need to prefix an ampersand symbol to the variable name, which is something you must remember to do. You do not need to prefix the ampersand to a string or array, which is something you'll forget to do. The ampersand used here is the memory location operator, which is covered in a later chapter.

The code below demonstrates how to read an integer value from standard input:

```
1     #include <stdio.h>
2
3     int main()
4     {
5          int x;
6
7          printf("Type an integer: ");
8          scanf("%d", &x);
9          printf("Integer %d\n", x);
10
11         return(0);
12   }
13
```

The scanf() function at line 8 uses the %d placeholder to fetch the integer value. It is assigned to variable *x*. See the ampersand; don't forget it. Build and run this code. Type an integer, which is any whole number. The program assigns that value to variable *x* and then displays the result.

Now, if you were to modify our sample code to read in a floating point value, you would have to make some changes. First, of course, would be to change the variable type at line 5 to a floating point value. Simply change *int* to *float*. Suddenly, the variable x becomes a floating point value.

In line 7, obviously, we need to change the name integer. At line 8, change %d to %f for a floating point value. Finally at line 9, change the word integer, as well as the placeholder.

```
1       #include <stdio.h>
2
3       int main()
4       {
5               float x;
6
7               printf("Type a floating point value: ");
8               scanf("%f", &x);
9               printf("Floating point value %f\n", x);
10
11              return(0);
12      }
13
```

Save, build and run the code. Type a real number, such as 45.6. As you can see, the value is read and displayed. Don't freak out if you see a value that's not exactly 45.6. If you see something like 45.599998, know that this is what's called a precision error. Computers approximate real numbers, which is acceptable. In a later chapter, we'll show you how to fix the output to make it look more agreeable.

You could also modify the code so that it reads in a single character value. The changes are the same. First, you change the variable type from float to a single character variable at line 5. At line 7, change the prompt so that is says "Type a character." At line 8, change the percent placeholder in the *scanf()* function to a 'c' from an 'f,' to read in a single character value. Don't forget to change the prompt and placeholder at line 9.

With the variable x being a character variable, you need the %c placeholders to read in the proper values.

```
1       #include <stdio.h>
2
3       int main()
4       {
5               char x;
6
7               printf("Type a character: ");
8               scanf("%c", &x);
9               printf("Character %c\n", x);
10
```

```
11              return(0);
12      }
13
```

Save the changes, and then build and run the code. You could also use the *scanf()* function to read in strings, but you'll find peculiarities in this operation. Take a look at the code below:

```
1       #include <stdio.h>
2
3       int main()
4       {
5               char name[15];
6
7               printf("Your name? ");
8               scanf("%s", name);
9               printf("You are %s.\n", name);
10
11              return(0);
12      {
13
```

On line 5, the name variable is created. It has room to store 14 characters, plus one additional character for the null at the end of the string. The scanf() function at line 8 uses the %s placeholder to read in a string. The variable name is used without the ampersand. That's because *name* is a character array, and arrays do not require the ampersand operator. Build and run this code.

In the terminal window that appears, type your name and press the Enter key. As you can see, the string is read and displayed.

Now, for the peculiarities. Run the program again. This time, assume that your name is Jerry Bob, which are two words. The scanf() function stops reading characters at the first white space character—a space, tab, or new line. There's no way you can force scanf() to read in those characters. It is just the way it works. Basically, scanf() is really a string input function where the strings are just one world long.

A better function to use for reading strings is *fgets*. *Fgets* is a file input function that can also be used to read standard input. Take a look at the code below:

```
1       #include <stdio.h>
2
3       int main()
4       {
5               char input[64];
6
7               printf("Instructions: ");
8               fgets(input,64,stdin);
9               puts("Thank you! Here are your instructions:");
10              puts(input);
11
12              return(0);
13      }
14
```

The variable *input* is created at line 5. It has room for 63 characters, plus one for the null character at the end of the string. The *fgets* function at line 8 reads standard input. The first argument is the variable into which the input is stored. This location is also called a buffer, which is just nerd jargon for storage.

The second argument indicates the size of the buffer. Again, 64 is used. That's 63 characters plus the null character at the end. The final argument is *stdin*, which is standard input. The *puts* function at line 10 reads the stored text and sends it to standard output. Build and run this code.

At the terminal window that appears, type your instructions. Press Enter, and then you will see your string, spaces, and everything.

CHAPTER 6: MATH OPERATORS

The important thing to remember when it comes to math and programming is that the computer does the work. You just have to copy the equation down properly. To do so, you need to know a few math operators, plus some other C language rules and procedures. In this chapter, we will review the basic Math operators and how they are used. Also explored are the increment and decrement operators, plus a few notes on the order of precedence, which determines which part of an equation is evaluated first.

The C language uses four basic symbols for the four basic math operators: addition, subtraction, multiplication, and division. These should be familiar to you, especially if you've used spreadsheets. The asterisk is used for multiplication, and that's because symbol is not available on the keyboard; please don't use the letter x.

Similarly, the division symbol is not found on the standard computer keyboard, so a slash is used instead. Two additional operators are increment and decrement. These are single operators despite using two characters. These operators serve a useful purpose when dealing with loops, which is a topic covered in a later chapter.

Math Operators:
- +   Addition
- -   Subtraction
- *   Multiplication
- /   Division

Additional math operators:

- ++   Increment, to add one to a variable
- - -   Decrement, to subtract one to a variable

Remember:

- Use * instead of x
- Use / instead of ÷

In C, the calculation goes on the right. The result is then assigned to a variable on the left. Or the result could be used immediately, as in the *printf* function show below:

- var = 888 + 111;
- printf("That's %d months!\n", age * 12);

Take a look at the code below:

```
1       #include <stdio.h>
2
3       int main()
4       {
5               int a;
6               int b = 5;
7
8               printf("Input an integer: ");
9               scanf("%d", &a);
10              printf("%d + %d = %d\n", a,b,a+b);
11
12              return(0);
13      }
14
15
```

Two variables are declared: *a* and *b*. In line 6, we've preset the value of variable *b* to 5. The *scanf* function at line 9 reads an integer value and stores it in variable *a*. Then, the *printf* function at line 10 displays both value—*a* and *b*—as well as their sum. The math equation is the third argument in the *printf* function. Now, build and run this code.

Type in a value to see the sum of that value and 5. To change addition to subtraction, you need to make only one modification. Look at the code above for a second and see if you can spot the place where that modification could take place.

To change addition to subtraction, simply change the math operator between *a* and *b* at line 10. Also, change the operator between the display strings—between the two %*ds*--so that it matches the output when you run the code. Now, build and run the code.

You'll notice that negative values are calculated as well. If you wanted to try multiplication, again you need to change the math operators. Look at the code example below to see where the changes took place:

```
1       #include <stdio.h>
2
3       int main()
4       {
5               int a;
6               int b = 5;
```

```
7
8              printf("Input an integer: ");
9              scanf("%d", &a);
10             printf("%d * %d = %d\n",a,b,a*b);
11
12             return(0);
13   }
14
15
```

As you can see, it took place between the two *%d*s and between the variables *a* and *b* at line 10. Now save the code, build, and then run.

The final modification, as you've probably guessed, is division. Division can be a little bit tricky, especially with integer values. Let's take a look. Go ahead and change the math operators in the *printf* statement at line 10. That's the only change that we're going to make:

```
1      #include <stdio.h>
2
3      int main()
4      {
5              int a;
6              int b = 5;
7
8              printf("Input an integer: ");
9              scanf("%d", &a);
10             printf("%d / %d = %d\n",a,b,a/b);
```

```
11
12              return(0);
13      }
14
15
```

Save, build, and run the code. Type in an integer value, such as *9*. The result that will be displayed is *1*, which is dubious. To do division properly, you need to use floating point values. Take a look at the code below:

```
1       #include <stdio.h>
2
3       int main()
4       {
5               float a;
6               float b = 5.0;
7
8               printf("Input an integer: ");
9               scanf("%f", &a);
10              printf("%f / %d = %f\n",a,b,a/b);
11
12              return(0);
13      }
14
15
```

This is basically a modification of existing code, switching values from *int* to *float*, as well as the associated placeholders. The value

5.0 is assigned to variable *b* at line 6. Remember, floating points have a decimal part. When you're writing a whole number, you need to specify a ".0" after the value. Now build and run the code.

Try the value *9* again. The result is more palatable, but ugly. In a later chapter, we'll discuss how to clean up the output of floating point values. Now take a look at the code below:

```
1       #include <stdio.h>
2
3       int main()
4       {
5               int x = 10;
6
7               printf("%d\n",x);
8               x = x + 1;
9               printf("%d\n",x);
10
11              return(0);
12      }
13
```

Math is present at line 8. It adds one to the value of variable *x*. This equation may look funky to you, but it's how it works. The compiler calculates the right side of the equation first. 1 is added to the value of variable *x*. That result is then stored back to the value of variable *x*. To prove how it works, build and run the code.

The original value is *10*, and the modified value is *11*. You can manipulate every single variable in this manner. Common manipulation is to add or subtract 1 in the variable's value. For example, if you want to increment the value of variable *x* by *1*, you use the increment operator, which is two plus signs "++" in a row. Change line 8 in the code to read:

```
8                    x++
```

The code above is a statement by itself; it is a mathematical operation. Save and run the code. The decrement operator is two minus signs "- -". Edit the code again to replace the increment operator with the decrement operator. Now save, build and run. As you can see from the output, it'll show the original value, which is *10*, and the modified decremented value, which is *9*.

The final math goodie that we would like to show you deals with what's called as the order of precedence. It involves math equations that have multiple operators. Take a look at the code below:

```
1        #include <stdio.h>
2
3        int main()
4        {
5                int a;
6
7                a = 25 / 5 * 2 + 3;
8                printf("The answer is %d\n",a);
9
10               return(0);
11       }
12
```

Can you guess the value of variable *a* just by looking at line 7? Run the code to see what the computer thinks. The computer thinks the answer is *13*. The reason behind this is that division and multiplication are prioritized over subtraction and addition. Also, the equation is executed starting from the left going to the right. So *25* divided by *5*, is *5*. *5* multiplied by *2* is *10*, and *10* plus *3* is *13*.

You can change the order of precedence using parenthesis. For example, let's enclose 2 + 3 in a parenthesis. This means that that part of the equation is evaluated first.

```
1       #include <stdio.h>

3       int main()
4       {
5               int a;

7               a = 25 / 5 * (2 + 3);
8               printf("The answer is %d\n",a);

10              return(0);
11      }
12
```

Save, build, and run the code. Now the answer is *25*—2 plus 3 is 5, 25 divided by 5 is 5, and 5 multiplied by 5 is 25. Now, let's add more parentheses. Remember to match them up.

```
1       #include <stdio.h>

3       int main()
```

```
4      {
5              int a;
6
7              a = 25 / (5 * (2 + 3));
8              printf("The answer is %d\n",a);
9
10             return(0);
11     }
12
```

Now, the answer is *1*. That's because *2* plus *3* is *5*, *5* multiplied by *5* is *25*, and *25* divided by *25* is *1*. Remember that in C, multiplication and division are evaluated first, then addition and subtraction. This is how equations are evaluated, unless you use parenthesis to modify the order of precedence.

MATH LIBRARY FUNCTIONS

When you can't find an operator to do your math, you need to turn to the C library. There you'll find fun and friendly functions to sate your mathematical whims. In this section, we cover two of the typical C language math library functions: the square root function and the power function. We'll also discuss the random number generating function, which isn't really a math function, but it's something you may find quite handy.

To generate the square root of a value, you use the *sqrt* function. It reads like "sqrt," but it's really "square root." The square root function is shown at line 8 in the code below:

```
1       #include <stdio.h>
2       #include <math.h>
3
4       int main()
5       {
6               float r;
7
8               r = sqrt(2.0);
9
10              printf("The square root of 2 is %f\n",r);
11
12              return(0);
13      }
14
```

As you can see in line 2, it requires the math.h header file. The function swallows a floating point value specified as *2.0*. It returns the square root as a floating point value, which is saved in the float variable *r*. The *printf* function at line 10 displays the result. Build and run this code.

Now, you know the square root of *2,* or any other value that you specify in the code. Another math function worthy of note is the *pow* function, which is short for "power." The C language lacks a power operator, which is common in other programming languages, but the *pow* function is far more versatile. Take a look at the code below:

```
1       #include <stdio.h>
2       #include <math.h>
3
```

```
4        int main()
5        {
6                float p;
7
8                p = pow(2.0,8.0);
9
10               printf("2 to the 8th power is %f\n",p);
11
12               return(0);
13       }
14
```

The pow function appears at line 8. It also required the math.h header file, which is shown in line 2. The pow function uses two arguments, both of which are floating point values. The first value is the base, the second is the exponent. So here, *2.0* is being raised to the 8th power. The result is saved in floating point variable *p*, and then it is printed in line 10. Build and run the code.

2 to the 8th power is 256. Generally speaking, all C language math functions require the inclusion of the math.h header file. They all work with real numbers. We used floating point numbers in our previous example, but officially they should be double-type variables. The double carries twice the precisions of a float. That means, it is more accurate. But it should really be used only when a greater degree of precision is required.

Another popular math function, although it is not a true math function, is *rand*. It generates pseudo-random numbers. It is called "pseudo" because they can be predicted. However, they're still good enough to be random in a general sense. The *rand* function requires the stdlib.h, or standard library header file, for its definition. This is the most common header file after stdio.h. Take a look at the code below:

```
1       #include <stdio.h>
2       #include <stdlib.h>
3
4       int main()
5       {
6               int r;
7
8               r = rand();
9
10              printf("%d is a random number.\n",r);
11
12              return(0);
13      }
14
```

The function itself requires no arguments. It simply generates a random integer value. That value is stored in variable *r* at line 8 of the above code. The *printf* function at line 10 displays the result. Build and run the code.

For the rand function to work best, you must 'seed' the randomizer. That's a software machine that generates random numbers. The random seeding function is called *srand*, which is also defined in the stdlib.h header file. In the code, insert the *srand* function in the line above *rand* like so:

```
1       #include <stdio.h>
2       #include <stdlib.h>
3
4       int main()
5       {
6               int r;
7
8               srand(66);
9               r = rand();
10
11              printf("%d is a random number.\n",r);
12
13              return(0);
14      }
15
```

The *srand* function requires a positive integer argument to seed the randomizer. In our example, we're using the number 66. Save the changes, and then build and run the code. This time, a new random number appears. But will the same value appear when you run the code for the second time? Go ahead and see.

Mostly likely, you will see the same number. Now don't be alarmed, there's nothing wrong with your code. You have several tools available to reseed the randomizer. One is that you could ask the user to input a positive integer value when the program starts. What most programmers do is borrow the current tick-tock value from the computer's internal time clock. We'll cover time functions in a later chapter. For now, we need to change line 8 of the code to replace the value 66 with a time function.

We need to type—in parenthesis—the word 'unsigned,' and then the time function, and then in its parenthesis you need to put the word 'NULL' in all caps like so:

```
1      #include <stdio.h>
2      #include <stdlib.h>
3
4      int main()
5      {
6              int r;
7
8              srand((unsigned)time(NULL));
9              r = rand();
10
11             printf("%d is a random number.\n",r);
12
13             return(0);
14     }
15
```

Make sure that all parenthesis matches up. Yes, this looks odd. But it is important that the parenthesis match—one set around 'unsigned' and one set around 'NULL,' and then one set around the whole thing, which is the *srand* function.

What this function does, is to fetch the current tick-tock value from the computer's clock. It is a number that's constantly changing. Save the code and run it. Now you'll see a new value. Run the code again. This time you'll see a new value. Don't be surprised if the resulting values are close to each other. Keep in mind that it is based on the 'seconds' value of the computer clock, which is incrementing throughout the day.

Why are random numbers so important? Because random numbers are the key to making all computer games interesting.

CHAPTER 7: C LANGUAGE COMPARISONS

Generally speaking, a program executes statements as they appear in the source code, one line after the other. To change that order is to alter that program's flow. One of the most common flow control words in the C language is *if*, which is similar to its human language counterpart also called *if*. In this chapter, we introduce you to the *if* keyword. You'll also discover how comparisons are made in the C language, as well as how to handle multiple decisions.

IF STATEMENTS

Before you can use the *if* keyword, you must understand how comparisons work in C. Two values or expressions are evaluated. To make that evaluation, you use one of the C language's comparison operators. Here are the most common comparison operators:

-
- == "Is equal to"
- > "Greater than"
- < "Lesser than"
- <= "Less than or equal to"
- >= "Greater than or equal to"
- != "Does not equal"

Take a look at the code below:

```
1        #include <stdio.h>
2
```

```
3       int main();
4       {
5               int a;
6
7               printf("Type an integer: ");
8               scanf("%d",&a);
9               printf("You typed %d.\n",a);
10              if(a > 10)
11                      printf("%d is greater than 10.\n",a);
12
13              return(0);
14      }
15
```

The user is prompted to type an integer value. The value is displayed at line 9. At line 10, an *if* statement evaluates that value. If the value is greater than 10, line 11 is executed. Otherwise, line 11 is skipped. Now build and run this code.

Type in any integer value. For the sake of this example, we'll type in the number *50*. As you can see, it worked. The output displays the *printf* statement indicated at line 11. Now try typing a value that is lesser than *10*. As you can see, the program terminates and line 11 is ignored.

An if statement is traditionally formatted differently from other statements. It is split between two or more lines. The first line sets the *if* condition in parenthesis. If that condition is evaluated as true, the next line is executed. Actually, it is just one statement split between two lines. See how the semi-colon is at the end of line 11 and not at line 10.

You could also write it as a single line, but that's uncommon. More common is to enclose the statements belonging to if in curly brackets like this:

```
1      #include <stdio.h>
2
3      int main();
4      {
5              int a;
6
7              printf("Type an integer: ");
8              scanf("%d",&a);
9              printf("You typed %d.\n",a);
10             if(a > 10)
11             {
12                     printf("%d is greater than 10.\n",a);
13             }
14
15             return(0);
16     }
17
```

This format is actually required when more than one statement is executed based on the *if* condition. For example, let's move line 9 of the code down to line 12. Save, build, and run the code.

```
1        #include <stdio.h>

2

3        int main();

4        {

5                int a;

6

7                printf("Type an integer: ");

8                scanf("%d",&a);

9                if(a > 10)

10               {

11                       printf("You typed %d.\n",a);

12                       printf("%d is greater than 10.\n",a);

13               }

14

15               return(0);

16       }

17
```

Type in the number 25, for example. Now since the number is greater than 10, both lines are now displayed. Take a look at the code below:

```
1        #include <stdio.h>

2

3        int main();

4        {

5                int a;

6

7                printf("Type an integer: ");
```

```
8              scanf("%d",&a);
9              printf("You typed %d.\n",a);
10             if(a > 10)
11             {
12                     printf("%d is greater than 10.\n",a);
13             }
14             if(a < 10)
15             {
16                     printf("%d is lesser than 10.\n",a);
17             }
18
19             return(0);
20     }
```

This code shows two *if* comparisons in a row. Each of which has its own set of curly brackets. Two conditions are evaluated: greater than at line 10 and less than at line 14. Build and run the code.

As you can see after running the code, the appropriate output is displayed for values lesser or greater than 10 that you typed in. However, notice that you won't see the appropriate output when you type *10* itself.

Edit line 14 so that "Less than or equal to" is used as the operator. Edit line 16 to reflect the same results like so:

```
1      #include <stdio.h>
2
3      int main();
```

```
4        {
5                int a;
6
7                printf("Type an integer: ");
8                scanf("%d",&a);
9                printf("You typed %d.\n",a);
10               if(a > 10)
11               {
12                       printf("%d is greater than 10.\n",a);
13               }
14               if(a <= 10)
15               {
16                       printf("%d is lesser than or equal to
10.\n",a);
17               }
18
19               return(0);
20       }
```

Save, build, and run the code.

ELSE STATEMENTS

Another way to handle an either or decision, is to use the keyword
else. Take a look at the code below:

```
1        #include <stdio.h>
2
3        int main()
4        {
```

```
5              int a;

6

7              printf("Type an integer: ");

8              scanf("%d", &a);

9              printf("You otyped %d.\n",a);

10             if(a > 10)

11             {

12                     printf("%d is greater than 10.\n",a);

13             }

14             else

15             {

16                     printf("%d is less than or equal to
10.\n",a);

17             }

18

19             return(0);

20     }

21
```

This code is a rewrite of our previous code, but it uses the *else* keyword. The *if* condition at line 10 makes an evaluation. Its statements are executed when that condition is true. If the condition is false, the statements belonging to *else* are executed instead. Build and run this code.

Note that else doesn't have a semi-colon. Instead, it has curly brackets. All could be written without brackets because it's only followed by one statement.

ELSE IF STATEMENTS

When three or more conditions are present, you can evaluate them using an *else if* structure. Take a look at the code below:

```
1       #include <stdio.h>
2
3       int main()
4       {
5               int a;
6
7               printf("Type an integer: ");
8               scanf("%d", &a);
9               printf("You otyped %d.\n",a);
10              if(a > 10)
11              {
12                      printf("%d is greater than 10.\n",a);
13              }
14              else if(a < 10)
15              {
16                      printf("%d is less than or equal to
10.\n",a);
17              }
18              else
19              {
20                      printf("%d is 10.\n",a);
21              }
22              return(0);
23      }
24
```

This structure starts with an *if* statement at line 10. When that condition is true, those statements belonging to that condition are executed, and the rest are skipped over. Otherwise, a second condition—*else if*—is examined at line 14. If that condition is true, its statements are executed and the rest are skipped over. At the end of the structure is an *else* all by itself. Its statements are executed when the preceding conditions aren't met. Build and run this code.

The result is similar to the previous examples. Except this time, when a value of *10* is typed, the *printf* statement under *else* statement is executed. You can have as many *else if* statements stacked up as you like, which helps evaluate complex situations.

A reminder: the *if, else if,* and *else* keywords are generally not immediately followed by a semi-colon. In the C language, a semi-colon by itself is a statement. When one lingers after an *if* evaluation, the compiler believes that the semi-colon is the statement, and that not anything follows it. This is a common mistake by novice programmers. Take a look at the code below:

```
1       #include <stdio.h>
2
3       int main()
4       {
5               int a = -5;
6
7               if(a > 0);
8                       printf("%d is a positive
number.\n",a);
```

```
9
10              return(0);
11    }
12
13
```

Build and run. Obviously, negative 5 is not positive number. Now if you're using the Clong compiler, you can click on the Build log tab and review a specific error message. Other compilers are not as smart. To fix the problem, simply remove the semi-colon dangling at the end of line 7. Save, build, and run the code.

```
1      #include <stdio.h>
2
3      int main()
4      {
5              int a = -5;
6
7              if(a > 0)
8                      printf("%d is a positive
number.\n",a);
9
10              return(0);
11    }
12
13
```

No output means that negative 5 fails the condition. Remember, the semi-colon goes after the statement, not after the parenthesis that holds *if's* condition.

SWITCH/ELSE STATEMENTS

The C language lets you handle complex decisions by stacking a bunch of *if/else* conditions. Sometimes, that structure can get a bit ugly. As an alternative, you can employ the *switch/case* structure, which is yet another decision making tool in the C language.

In this section, we'll talk about the *switch/case* structure. You'll see how it is constructed, how it can handle multiple decisions, plus we'll talk about a few tricks. Take a look at the code below:

```
1       #include <stdio.h>
2
3       int main()
4         {
5               char a;
6
7               printf("Your choice (1,2,3): ");
8               scanf("%c", &a);
9
10              switch(a)
11                {
12                      case '1':
13                              puts("Excellent choice!");
14                              break;
15                      case '2':
16                              puts("This is the most
common choice: ");
17                              break;
18                      case '3':
```

96

```
19                      puts("I questions your
judgement.");
20                          break;
21                  default:
22                          puts("That's not a valid
choice.");
23          }
24
25          return(0);
26    }
27
28
```

The bulk of this code is a *switch*/*case* structure. It starts with a *switch* at line 10. This is followed by a series of *case* statements, each of which has its own statements. The final piece is the default. It is followed by its own statements as well, and then a closing curly bracket. These are the elements of the *switch*/*case* structure.

The *switch*/*case* structure also makes use of the *break* keyword. So all in all, this structure contains four C language keywords: *switch*, *case*, *default*, and *break*. Build and run the code above to see what it does. Run it a few times to try out various options. The code accepts character input, although it could have easily accepted integers.

Here's how it works: Switch handles a single value, not a comparison. It can be a mathematical equation, but the result must be a single value. That value, specified by *switch*, is then compared to the values of each *case* statement. If the comparison is true, then the statements belonging to the *case* statement that is flagged as true is executed. If not, they're skipped.

At line 12, if the character *1* is typed, then the *puts* statement at line 13 is executed. The break at line 14 ends the switch case evaluation, returning control to the line after the switch structure's final curly bracket, which is at line 23. Otherwise, if a match isn't made, execution falls to the next *case* statement, and then the next, and so forth.

Finally, the *default* condition is executed when none of the *case* conditions match. It doesn't need a *break* statement as it is the end of the structure. Modify the code by commenting out all the *break* statements. Insert double slashes at line 14, 17, and line 20.

```
1       #include <stdio.h>

3       int main()
4       {
5               char a;

7               printf("Your choice (1,2,3): ");
8               scanf("%c", &a);

10              switch(a)
11              {
12                      case '1':
13                              puts("Excellent choice!");
14//                          break;
```

```
15                     case '2':
16                             puts("This is the most common choice: ");
17//                            break;
18                     case '3':
19                             puts("I questions your judgement.");
20//                            break;
21                  default:
22                             puts("That's not a valid choice.");
23              }
24
25              return(0);
26      }
27
28
```

Save the changes, and then build and run the code. If you type a character other than 1, 2, or 3, you see the invalid choice message displayed. But type a '1,' you'll see all the messages displayed. That is because execution falls through to each *case* statement. Take a look at the code below:

```
1       #include <stdio.h>
2
3       int main()
4       {
5               char a;
```

```
6
7               puts("Vacation options: ");
8               puts("A – Airfare");
9               puts("B – Hotel");
10              puts("C – Rental Car");
11              scanf("%c", &a);
12
13              switch(a)
14              {
15                      case 'A':
16                              puts("You have selected the
airfare");
17                              break;
18                      case 'B':
19                              puts("You have selected
Hotel");
20                              break;
21                      case 'C':
22                              puts("You have selected
Rental Car");
23                              break;
24                      default:
25                              puts("That is an invalid
choice");
26              }
27
28              return(0);
29
30      }
31
32
```

Here's another switch/case structure, one that evaluates input as a menu system. Build and run the code. The problem with these options is that you may have typed a small 'a' instead of a big 'A.' In that case, the program doesn't seem to behave properly. Address the issue by adjusting the case statements to account for both upper and lowercase input.

Edit the source code to add duplicate *case* statements for the lower case letters like so:

```
1       #include <stdio.h>
2
3       int main()
4       {
5               char a;
6
7               puts("Vacation options: ");
8               puts("A – Airfare");
9               puts("B – Hotel");
10              puts("C – Rental Car");
11              scanf("%c", &a);
12
13              switch(a)
14              {
15                      case 'A':
16                              puts("You have selected the airfare");
17                              break;
18                      case 'a':
```

```
19                    puts("You have selected the
airfare");
20                        break;
21            case 'B':
22                        puts("You have selected
Hotel");
23                        break;
24            case 'b':
25                        puts("You have selected
Hotel");
26                        break;
27            case 'C':
28                        puts("You have selected
Rental Car");
29                        break;
30            case 'c':
31                        puts("You have selected
Rental Car");
32                        break;
33            default:
34                        puts("That is an invalid
choice")
35          }
36
37          return(0);
38    }
39
40
```

Save the changes and then build and run the code. Now the evaluation should work for both upper and lower case letters. As you can see, the number of lines of code is significantly increased. Here's another way to write the code so that it'll accept both upper and lower case letters, and lessen the number of lines of code a little bit.

```
1       #include <stdio.h>
2
3       int main()
4       {
5               char a;
6
7               puts("Vacation options: ");
8               puts("A – Airfare");
9               puts("B – Hotel");
10              puts("C – Rental Car");
11              scanf("%c", &a);
12
13              switch(a)
14              {
15                      case 'A':
16                      case 'a':
17                              puts("You have selected the
airfare");
18                              break;
19                      case 'B':
20                      case 'b':
21                              puts("You have selected
Hotel");
```

```
22                              break;
23                   case 'C':
24                   case 'c':
25                              puts("You have selected
Rental Car");
26                              break;
27                   default:
28                              puts("That is an invalid
choice");
29         }
30
31         return(0);
32    }
33
34
```

You can also address this problem by using C language functions that modify character case. That topic is covered in another chapter. Another way that program flow can be altered is when one or more statements are repeated over and over. This process is referred to as a *loop*.

THE *WHILE* LOOP

The C language offers several ways of looping. In this section we will discuss the *while* type of loop. You'll learn how to setup the loop, determine when to stop looping, and how to break out of a loop before it is done.

A loop is a repetitive way to control program execution. You must specify a condition that makes the loop repeat, a set of statements that repeat, and a way for the loop to stop. In the code below, a *while* loop counts from *1* to *10*.

```
1       #include <stdio.h>
2
3       int main()
4       {
5               int x;
6
7               x = 1;
8               while(x <= 10)
9               {
10                      printf("%d\n",x);
11                      x++;
12              }
13
14              return(o);
15      }
16
17
```

The looping condition is specified at line 8. It reads that while the value of variable x is less than or equal to 10—as long as that condition is true—the statements in the loop between the curly brackets at line 9 and 12 will repeat. The value of x is initialized at line 7.

At line 11, the value of variable x is incremented. So as long as x is inching up, the loop repeats until *x* is greater than 10. Build and run the code, and you'll see the values from 1 through 10 displayed.

Now, let's say you wanted to count to 20. Can you imagine where in the source code you will have to make that change? It is simple: Change the condition in the *while* loop to 20, instead of 10. Save that change, and then build and run the code.

```
1       #include <stdio.h>
2
3       int main()
4       {
5               int x;
6
7               x = 1;
8               while(x <= 20)
9               {
10                      printf("%d\n",x);
11                      x++;
12              }
13
14              return(o);
15      }
16
17
```

Now, values 1 through 20 are displayed. Suppose instead of going by 1, you wanted to display only the even numbers from 2 to 20. This requires a little bit more thought because it changes two things: the initialization and how the value of variable *x* increases.

The first change is to initialize the variable *x* to *2* at line 7. If you're going to be counting by 2s, so start at 2. Then, modify line 11 so that the value of x is incremented by 2, which is not really an increment; it's a mathematical function. *x* equals the value of *x* plus *2*.

```
1       #include <stdio.h>
2
3       int main()
4       {
5               int x;
6
7               x = 2;
8               while(x <= 20)
9               {
10                      printf("%d\n",x);
11                      x = x + 2;
12              }
13
14              return(o);
15      }
16
17
```

Save, build and run the code. There you will see the even numbers between *2* and *20*. It is also possible for loops to count backwards. If you were to count backwards, say from 10 to 1, can you think of how you would modify the code so that that would happen? Obviously, there are a few changes that would need to be made.

If you are going to start at 10, you need to change the initial value to 10. Then, the condition needs to change as well, because already, the loop wouldn't repeat. The condition should be: while *x* is greater than zero. Then the statement at line 11 needs to be changed as well. The value of *x* should be decremented each time the loop spins.

```
1       #include <stdio.h>
2
3       int main()
4       {
5               int x;
6
7               x = 10;
8               while(x > 0)
9               {
10                      printf("%d\n",x);
11                      x --;
12              }
13
14              return(0);
15      }
16
17
```

Save, build and run the code. There, the loop counts from 10 to 1. Take a look at the code below:

```
1       #include <stdio.h>
2       #include <stdlib.h>
```

```
3       #include <time.h>

4

5       int main()

6       {

7               int x, r;

8

9               srand((unsigned)time(NULL));
/*Seed randomizer */

10

11              x = 10;

12              while(x > 0)

13              {

14                      r = rand();

15                      printf("%d\n", r);

16                      x--;

17              }

18

19              return(0);

20

21      }

22

23
```

This code uses the *srand* and *rand* functions introduced in the previous chapter. These functions generate random numbers. In this case, a *while* loop displays ten random numbers. Build and run the code. Let us now discuss a couple of tricks to clean up the numbers.

The first is the modulus operator, which is a percent '%' sign. Modulus calculates the remainder of a value like leftovers. In fact, take a look at the code below to see a demonstration:

```
1       #include <stdio.h>
2
3       int main()
4       {
5              int a, b;
6
7              a = 7;
8              while(a < 30)
9              {
10                    b = a % 7;                /* b equals a mode 7 */
11                    printf("%d %% 7 = %d\n",a,b);
12                    a++;
13             }
14             return(0);
15      }
16
17
```

Here, we're making use of a C program to teach you C. The *while* loop marches through the values 7 through 30. It shows you how the modulus operator affects each of those values. Build and run the code.

The modulus operator gives you a remainder. So for example, *10 %*

7 yields 3. That's because 7 goes into 10 once, but with 3 remainders. You can see how the value is always going to be between 0 and 6 for mod 7, no matter what the initial value is used.

Now in the code below, edit the value of line 15 so that the *printf* function displays the value of *r % 100*.

```
1        #include <stdio.h>
2        #include <stdlib.h>
3        #include <time.h>
4
5        int main()
6        {
7                int x, r;
8
9                srand((unsigned)time(NULL));
/*Seed randomizer */
10
11               x = 10;
12               while(x > 0)
13               {
14                       r = rand();
15                       printf("%d\n", r % 100);
16                       x--;
17               }
18
19               return(0);
20
21       }
22
23
```

This change limits the output to values between *0* and *99*. Save, build, and run the code. You may see some single digits in there. The single digits don't really look properly formatted. To line up the numbers, you can edit the *printf* statement again. This time, insert a '2' in the %d placeholder.

```
1        #include <stdio.h>
2        #include <stdlib.h>
3        #include <time.h>
4
5        int main()
6        {
7                int x, r;
8
9                srand((unsigned)time(NULL));
/*Seed randomizer */
10
11               x = 10;
12               while(x > 0)
13               {
14                       r = rand();
15                       printf("%2d\n", r % 100);
16                       x--;
17               }
18
19               return(0);
20
21       }
22
23
```

The '2' sets the width of integer output to two characters wide, right justified. Save, build and run the code. Now you'll see a single digit, but it is lined up on the right, which actually looks more pleasing.

DO/WHILE LOOP

Another type of loop is the Do/While loop. It is a kind of an upside down *while* loop, but it guarantees that the loop always executes at least once. Take a look at the code below:

```
1       #include <stdio.h>
2
3       int main()
4       {
5               char ch;
6
7               ch = 'A';
8
9               do
10              {
11                      putchar(ch);
12                      ch++;
13              }
14              while (ch != 'z');
15
16              putchar('\n');
17
18              return(0);
19      }
20
```

The *Do/While* loop starts at line 9 with a *Do* statement. It has no condition. Instead, the statements are executed one after the other. The while condition appears at line 14. The loop relies on variable *ch* as its condition. That variable is initialized at line 7, and then manipulated in line 12. Build and run the code.

The 'z' isn't printed because it's an exit condition. If you want to see the 'z,' you need to save the exit condition to 'z + 1' like so:

```
1       #include <stdio.h>
2
3       int main()
4       {
5               char ch;
6
7               ch = 'A';
8
9               do
10              {
11                      putchar(ch);
12                      ch++;
13              }
14              while (ch != 'z'+1);
15
16              putchar('\n');
17
18              return(0);
19      }
20
```

Save and run the code. This code below demonstrates an endless loop. There is no exit condition because the while loop's evaluation is always one.

```
1       #include <stdio.h>
2
3       int main()
4       {
5               while(1)
6               {
7                       printf("I'm endlessly looping! ");
8               }
9
10              return(0);
11      }
12
```

Build and run the code. Press *Ctrl* + *C* to cancel the program and stop the madness. Now, endless loops do have their place, but most of them are unintentional. You can, however, fix the loop by using the *break* statement. Insert a *break* statement at line 8 of the code above like so:

```
1       #include <stdio.h>
2
3       int main()
4       {
5               while(1)
6               {
7                       printf("I'm endlessly looping! ");
```

```
8                    break;
9               }
10
11              return(0);
12       }
13
```

Don't forget the semi-colon at the end of the *break* statement. Save, build and run the code. The loop spins only once because the *break* statement busts out of it. You can even use a break to bust out of a loop prematurely. Take a look at the code below:

```
1       #include <stdio.h>
2
3       int main()
4       {
5               int a = 0;
6
7               while(1)
8               {
9                       puts("Here I go....!");
10                      a++;
11                      if(a > 10)
12                              break;
13              }
14
15              return(0);
16      }
17
18
```

The *while* loop's condition is infinite, and it cannot change. The variable *a* is used to monitor the loops iterations. Once *a* is greater than *10*, the loop is busted. Build and run the code. Of course, a better solution would be to evaluate variable *a* at the *while* loop's parenthesis. That's something you can try on your own.

THE *FOR* KEYWORD

The *for* keyword is used for creating loops in your C code. Unlike the *while* loop, the *for* loop is setup on a single line, which makes it more cryptic. But it remains a more popular, or perhaps more traditional type of loop.

```
1       #include <stdio.h>
2
3       int main()
4       {
5               int x;
6
7               for(x=0;x<10;x++)
8                       printf("%d\n",x);
9
10              return(0);
11      }
12
13
```

In this section, we discuss the *for* loop. We will see how to setup the loop, and understand its parts. A *for* loop is presented at line 7. The loop's statement contains three parts, each separated by a semi-colon.

First is the initialization. The statement is '*x=0*,' which is an assignment that is made at the start of the loop. Second is the looping condition. The loop repeats as long as this condition is true: *x<10*. Finally, is the iteration statement. Each time the loop repeats, this statement is executed. Here, the value of *x* is incremented.

The semi-colon doesn't follow the *for* statement's parenthesis. Instead, the semi-colon follows a single looping statement, which is shown at line 8, or a series of statements are enclosed in curly brackets. Build and run the code. The values *0* through *9* are output. This is actually typical for a C loop. In C programming, you start counting at *0*, not *1*.

Humans start counting at *1*. To fix the loop for the human's eyes, change the *printf* statement at line 8 to read like so:

```
1      #include <stdio.h>
2
3      int main()
4      {
5              int x;
6
7              for(x=0;x<10;x++)
8                      printf("%d\n",x+1);
9
10              return(0);
11      }
12
13
```

This modification doesn't change the value of *x*, only the output. Save, build and run the code.

THE NESTED LOOP

The one thing that's great with a *for* loop is that you can make use of the concept of a nested loop. This is easier than using a *while* loop in C language. In this section, we'll talk about how to make a nested loop, as well as how to avoid the common looping pitfalls that programmers encounter in the C language. Take a look at the code below:

```
1       #include <stdio.h>
2       #include <stdlib.h>
3       #include <time.h>
4
5       int main()
6       {
7               int column, r;
8
9               srand((unsigned)time(NULL));        /* Seed
Randomizer */
10
11              for(column=0;column<10;column++)
12              {
13                      r = rand();
14                      printf("%2d\t",r % 100);
15              }
16              putchar('\n');
17
```

```
18              return(0);
19      }
20
21
```

The sample code that we have outputs ten randomly selected numbers. Build and run this code. As you can see from the output, there's now a row of ten randomly selected values. The spacing that's present in between each value is attained by making use of the tab character '\t,' which is at line 14 of the code.

Now, let's go ahead and try to make a 100 value grid. In addition to the single row of ten values that we already have, we need to create nine more rows of ten values. To accomplish this task, most C programmers use the nested loop, or a secondary *for* loop that repeats the output ten more times. Take a look at the code below:

```
1       #include <stdio.h>
2       #include <stdlib.h>
3       #include <time.h>
4
5       int main()
6       {
7               int row, column, r;
8
9               srand((unsigned)time(NULL));        /* Seed
Randomizer */
10
11              for(row=0;row<10;row++)
```

```
12                  {
13
for(column=0;column<10;column++)
14                      {
15                              r = rand();
16                              printf("%2d\t",r % 100);
17                      }
18              }
19          putchar('\n');
20
21          return(0);
22  }
23
24
```

The code above is a modified version of the code that we used earlier. It now has an extra loop. The column loop, which was the old loop, is now nested within a new loop called the row loop. The indentation that you see in the code is for readability--it helps match up the curly brackets of each statement. Build and run this code. As you can see, you now have a grid of 100 randomly selected values. Take a look at the code below:

```
1       #include <stdio.h>
2
3       int main()
4       {
5               int alpha, numeric;
6
```

```
7
8                    for(alpha='A';alpha<'K';alpha++)
9                        {
10
for(numeric=0;numeric<10;numeric++)
11
printf("%c%d\t",alpha,numeric);
12                              putchar('\n');
13                   }
14
15                   return(0);
16       }
17
18
```

The nested loop that you see above might be a little bit easier to read. The outer alpha loop sweeps through letters *A* through *J*; *K* is the limit. The inner loop loops from 0 to 9. You'll also notice that this inner loop does not make use of any curly brackets since it only contains one statement. At line 11, the loop variables are displayed. Build and run this code.

You can better observe how the nested loops execute in the output. First, loop *A*--the outer loop--executes. Then, the inner loop outputs the values 0 through 9. It is then follow by loop *B*, which also outputs 0 through 9, and so forth. Take a look at the code below:

```
1       #include <stdio.h>

2

3       int main()

4       {

5               char ch, t;

6

7               printf("Type a letter 'a' to 'z': ");

8               scanf("%c",$ch);

9

10              for(t='a';t<='z';t++)

11              {

12                      putchar(t);

13              }

14              putchar('\n');

15

16              return(0);

17      }

18

19
```

Input is prompted and then the alphabet is displayed. What we'd like you to think about doing is how to stop the loop when the letter input is equal to variable *t* in the loop. You don't need to change the four statements to make that happen. Instead, you need to put statements within the loop that would bust out of the loop when the character is input.

The key is to use an *if* test and follow that with a *break* statement. Take a look at the solution below:

```
1       #include <stdio.h>

2

3       int main()

4       {

5               char ch, t;

6

7               printf("Type a letter 'a' to 'z': ");

8               scanf("%c",$ch);

9

10              for(t='a';t<='z';t++)

11              {

12                      putchar(t);

13                      if( t == ch )

14                              break;

15              }

16              putchar('\n');

17

18              return(0);

19      }

20

21
```

At line 13, add *if(t == ch)* and then *break*. If you don't put the two equal signs in there, what you get is an assignment. In C, assignments always evaluate true. Don't forget about the semi-colon after the break statement. Save, build and run the code.

Remember to check these two items in a *for* statement: the looping condition and the iteration. If either is off, the loop would go on forever. The compiler doesn't check for flaws in logic. That's your job. A good tip is to read the *for* statement. Set t equal to character a. While t is less than or equal to character z, increment t.

If you change the condition to just $t=z$ for example, it would evaluate true and the loop would run forever. So watch your conditions and your iterations.

CHAPTER 8: ANATOMY OF A FUNCTION

The C library is brimming with functions. These functions do a lot of things, but perhaps not everything you need for your programs. Therefore, when necessary, you can concoct your own C language functions. In fact, most programmers have dozens, if not hundreds of their own functions.

In this chapter, we introduce you to the function. You'll see how to setup and prototype a function, how to call or access the function, and how to bail out of a function early. Like everything in the C language, a function has a certain style, and various etiquettes must be followed to add a function to your code.

A function has a type, a name, and arguments in parenthesis. A *type* is a value returned by the function—its output. The *name* is a unique name that identifies the function. The *arguments* are zero, one, or more values passed to the function—its input. Below, the alpha function has no input or output, which is valid in the C language. Therefore, it is a void function.

void alpha(void)

Void is a variable type, which means "I have no variable type." Function count is an integer function. It generates or returns integer values. It requires more input, and therefore has no arguments.

int count(void)

Function hangUp returns no values, so it's a void function. It does, however, accept a single character as input. The character is an argument. It is reference by variable *ch*. Before you can use a function, it must be introduced to the compiler. That way the compiler can check its arguments to ensure that it is being used properly.

Functions are called by their name, and then a parenthesis. When a function is called, control passes to the function's statements. Then, when the function is over, flow continues with the statement after the function call. The code below contains two functions:

```
1       #include <stdio.h>
2
3       void blorf(void);
4
5       int main ()
6       {
7               puts("The main () function always runs
first");
8               blorf();
9               puts("Thanks, blorf()");
10
11              return(0);
12      }
13
```

The main function is required in every C program. You also see the *blorf* function. Line 3 prototypes the *blorf* function. This informs the compiler of the function type and arguments. The compiler can confirm that the function is being used properly by checking the prototype. Also, the prototype is a statement. It ends in a semi-colon.

Line 8 calls the function. It has no arguments, so the parenthesis is empty. The function itself is found at line 14. This is effectively a repeat of the prototype minus the semi-colon. The statements belonging to the function are enclosed in curly brackets. Now build and run the code.

To call the function again, you simply specify it again. Duplicate line 8 to line 9.

```
1       #include <stdio.h>

2

3       void blorf(void);

4

5       int main ()

6       {

7               puts("The main () function always runs
first");

8               blorf();

9               blorf();

10              puts("Thanks, blorf()");

11

12              return(0);

13      }

14
```

Save, build and run the code. As you can see, the output appears twice. The prototype works like a definition for the function, describing how to use it before it appears in the code. You can avoid specifying a prototype, but only when you write the function before it is used. To see an example, take a look at the code below:

```
1       #include <stdio.h>
2
3       void soup(void);
4       {
5               puts("Pea green soup!");
6       }
7
8       int main()
9       {
10              printf("For breakfast I had ");
11              soup();
12              printf("For lunch I had ");
13              soup();
14
15              return(0);
16      }
17
18
```

The *sup* function appears above the *main* function. That's okay because the compiler still sees them in a function, and it is always the first function that is executed in the program. What is missing here is the prototype for the *sup* function. Build and run the code.

As you can see, the code outputs text as expected. But try this: move the *sup* function after the *main* function like so:

```
1       #include <stdio.h>
2
3
4       {
5               puts("Pea green soup!");
6       }
7
8       int main()
9       void soup(void);
10      {
11              printf("For breakfast I had ");
12              soup();
13              printf("For lunch I had ");
14              soup();
15
16              return(0);
17      }
18
19
```

Save and build the code. On most computers, you'll see one warning. Your compiler may report the misdeeds in a different manner. Either way, it is not good. You have to add the prototype. Go ahead and move *void soup(void)* above the main function.

```
1       #include <stdio.h>
2
3
4       {
5               puts("Pea green soup!");
6       }
7
8       void soup(void);
9       int main()
10
11      {
12              printf("For breakfast I had ");
13              soup();
14              printf("For lunch I had ");
15              soup();
16
17              return(0);
18      }
19
20
```

Now, there are no errors, and the output is the same as it originally was. Take a look at the code below:

```
1       #include <stdio.h>
2
3       void cheers(void);
4
5       int main()
```

```
6      {
7              puts("Everyone gets free dinner!");
8              cheers();
9              puts("Everyone gets free dessert!");
10             cheers();
11             puts("Everyone pays higher taxes!");
12
13             return(0);
14     }
15
16     void cheers(void);
17     {
18             int x;
19
20             for(x=0;x<3;x++)
21                     printf("Huzzah! ");
22             putcher('\n');
23     }
24
25
```

In this code, the *cheers* function contains its own variable—*x* at line 18. This variable is used only in the function here, to repeat the string three times. Build and run the code. You cannot reference variable *x* outside of its function. To prove it, insert a line above line 11 that displays its value.

```
1      #include <stdio.h>
2
```

```
3        void cheers(void);

4

5        int main()

6        {

7                puts("Everyone gets free dinner!");

8                cheers();

9                puts("Everyone gets free dessert!");

10               cheers();

11               printf("%d\n", x);

12               puts("Everyone pays higher taxes!");

13

14               return(0);

15       }

16

17       void cheers(void);

18       {

19               int x;

20

21               for(x=0;x<3;x++)

22                       printf("Huzzah! ");

23               putcher('\n');

24       }

25

26
```

Save the change and build. Don't even bother trying to run it because you won't be able to. The compiler is basically saying, "What the heck is *x*?" Now, try to define *x* and set its value inside the *main* function.

133

```
1       #include <stdio.h>
2
3       void cheers(void);
4
5       int main()
6       {
7               int x;
8
9               x=21;
10              puts("Everyone gets free dinner!");
11              cheers();
12              puts("Everyone gets free dessert!");
13              cheers();
14              printf("%d\n", x);
15              puts("Everyone pays higher taxes!");
16
17              return(0);
18      }
19
20      void cheers(void);
21      {
22              int x;
23
24              for(x=0;x<3;x++)
25                      printf("Huzzah! ");
26              putchar('\n');
27      }
28
29
```

Now save, build and run the code. The value of *x* in the main function is unaffected by the x variable in the *cheers* function. They are considered as two different variables. Here's another thing to remember: A function ends its run when its last statement is executed. In the *cheers* function, that's a *putchar* at line 26.

You can bail out of a function early by using the *return* keyword. Type *return;* at line 26.

```
1        #include <stdio.h>
2
3        void cheers(void);
4
5        int main()
6        {
7                int x;
8
9                x=21;
10               puts("Everyone gets free dinner!");
11               cheers();
12               puts("Everyone gets free dessert!");
13               cheers();
14               printf("%d\n", x);
15               puts("Everyone pays higher taxes!");
16
17               return(0);
18       }
19
20       void cheers(void);
```

```
21      {
22              int x;
23
24              for(x=0;x<3;x++)
25                      printf("Huzzah! ");
26              return;
27              putchar('\n');
28      }
29
30
```

You don't need to specify a value here because the *cheers* function is a *void* function—it doesn't return anything. In the main function, return must specify a value as it does at line 17, because *main* is an *int* function. Save the changes, and then build and run the code.

The output is messy because the *putchar* statement is skipped. That code is never executed because of the *return* statement right above it. More often you'll see a function return early based on a condition, which usually involves an *if* statement or a loop. Otherwise, anywhere the *return* is found marks the spot where the function bails out, and control returns to the calling function. Or, in the case of the main function, control is returned back to the operating system.

A function has got to *funct*; it is that I/O thing again. Sure, a void function is necessary and obviously valid, but most functions chew an input, and do something based on that input.

In this section, we'll talk about how functions can deal with arguments or values passed to the function. You'll see how to declare such a function, how it deals with values, and how to pass more than a single value to a function. The code below contains the repeat function, which accepts one argument—an integer.

```
1    #include <stdio.h>
2
3    void repeat(int count);
4
5    int main()
6    {
7            puts("At first the raven was like:");
8            repeat(1);
9            puts("But then he was all:");
10           repeat(5);
11
12           return(0);
13   }
14
15   void repeat(int count)
16   {
17           int x;
18
19           for(x=0;x<count;x++)
20                   puts("Nevermore!");
21   }
22
23
```

Within the function, the integer variable is named *count*. The function is called at lines 8 and 10, each time with a different argument. Inside the function, a local variable *x* is declared. It is used in the *for* statement, along with the *count* variable. Build and run the code.

The function can also accept integer variables as arguments. Make these modifications to the code:

- In the main function, declare integer variables *a* and *b*.
- Assign the value *1* to *a*, and *5* to *b*.
- Use a and b in the two *repeat* functions.

```
1        #include <stdio.h>
2
3        void repeat(int count);
4
5        int main()
6        {
7                int a, b;
8
9                a = 1;
10               b = 5;
11
12               puts("At first the raven was like:");
13               repeat(a);
14               puts("But then he was all:");
15               repeat(b);
16
17               return(0);
```

```
18        }
19
20        void repeat(int count)
21        {
22                int x;
23
24                for(x=0;x<count;x++)
25                        puts("Nevermore!");
26        }
27
28
```

Save the changes, and then build and run the code. As you can see, the output is the same. Take a look at the code below:

```
1        #include <stdio.h>
2
3        void product(float a, float b, float c);
4
5        int main()
6        {
7                float x,y,z;
8
9                printf("Type three numbers, separated by
spaces: ");
10                scanf("%f %f %f",&x,&y,&z);
11                product(x,y,z);
12
13                return(0);
```

```
14      }

15

16      void product(float a, float b, float c)

17      {

18          float p;

19

20          p = a * b * c;

21          printf("%f * %f *%f = %f\n",a,b,c,p);

22      }

23
```

In this code, you see a function that accepts three arguments. In this case, three floating-point values. The *scanf* function at line 10 reads in the three values. This is possible providing you format the input to match the format string. In the *product* function, the product of the three values is calculated and displayed. Build and run the code.

There is no limit to the number of arguments a function can accept. Although the more arguments, the more likely it will be to mess up the format. Functions don't necessarily need to eat all the same argument type either. Take a look at the code below:

```
1       #include <stdio.h>

2

3       void bar(char c, int count);

4

5       int main()

6       {

7           int x;
```

```
8
9               for(x=1;x<11;x++)
10                  bar('*',x*2);
11
12              return(0);
13      }
14
15      void bar(char c, int count)
16      {
17          int x;
18
19          for(x=0;x<count;x++)
20              putchar(c);
21          putchar('\n');
22      }
23
24
```

The *bar* function accepts two arguments: a character and an integer value. Build and run the code. The *bar* function uses both of its arguments to output a bar of a certain character across the display.

Most functions in the C library return a value. Even when that value isn't used, it's available. Returning a value allows functions to generate output. Most of the time, that output is based on the input or arguments passed to the function. In this section, we'll explain how functions return values. They can simply generate the information, or they can manipulate arguments to produce specific output.

We'll also cover a few rules and regulations regarding functions in the C language. The code below contains a function called *gimmeAnA.* It's a character function returning a *char* value. The function has no input according to its prototype at line 3.

```
1       #include <stdio.h>

2

3       char gimmeAnA(void);

4

5       int main()

6       {

7               char grade;

8

9               grade = gimmeAnA();

10              printf("On this test your received an
%c.\n",grade);

11

12              return(0);

13      }

14

15      char gimmeAnA(void)

16      {

17              return('A');

18      }

19

20
```

The function is called at line 9, where its return value is assigned to the *grade* variable. The function itself at line 15 merely returns the single character 'A.' Build and run this code.

When a function returns a value, the value can be used immediately. You can edit the code so that the *grade* variable is removed. First, delete the assignment, then replace the variable in *printf* with the *gimmeAnA* function.

```
1       #include <stdio.h>
2
3       char gimmeAnA(void);
4
5       int main()
6       {
7               printf("On this test your received an %c.\n",gimmeAnA());
8
9               return(0);
10      }
11
12
13      char gimmeAnA(void)
14      {
15              return('A');
16      }
17
18
```

Save the changes, and then build and run the code. As you can see, you still get an 'A' output. Take a look at the code below:

```c
1       #include <stdio.h>
2
3       float product(float a, float b, float c);
4
5       int main()
6       {
7               float a,x,y,z;
8
9               printf("Type three numbers, separated by
spaces: ");
10              scanf("%f %f %f",&x,&y,&z);
11              a = product(x,y,z);
12              printf("%f * %f * %f = %f\n",x,y,z,a);
13
14              return(0);
15      }
16
17      float product(float a, float b, float c)
18      {
19              float p;
20
21              p = a * b * c;
22              return(p);
23      }
24
25
```

In this code, the product function has been upgraded so that it returns the product of the values passed, which makes more sense.

Build and run the code. Type three values then press Enter to view their product.

The code can be cleaned up a bit. For example, variable *p* in the *product* function is not really needed. You can eliminate it to merely have the product returned.

```
1       #include <stdio.h>
2
3       float product(float a, float b, float c);
4
5       int main()
6       {
7               float a,x,y,z;
8
9               printf("Type three numbers, separated by
spaces: ");
10              scanf("%f %f %f",&x,&y,&z);
11              a = product(x,y,z);
12              printf("%f * %f * %f = %f\n",x,y,z,a);
13
14              return(0);
15      }
16
17      float product(float a, float b, float c)
18      {
19              return(a * b * c);
20      }
21
22
```

Save these changes, and then build and run the code. As you can see, the result is the same. A more realistic example is shown in the code below:

```
1       #include <stdio.h>
2
3       int max(int x, int y);
4       void isLarger(int big);
5
6       int main()
7       {
8               int a,b,larger;
9
10              printf("Type two integers separated by a
space: ");
11              scanf("%d %d",&a,&b);
12              larger = max(a,b);
13              if(a == larger)
14                      isLarger(a);
15              else
16                      isLarger(b);
17
18              return(0);
19      }
20
21      int max(int x, int y)
22      {
23              if(x > y)
24                      return(x);
```

```
25              return(y);
26      }
27
28      void isLarger(int big)
29      {
30              printf("Value %d is larger.\n",big);
31      }
32
33
```

Max is kind of the stalwart of learning C. It is passed two values, and returns the larger of the two. We've also added the *isLarger* function, which doesn't return anything, but we wanted to show how multiple function can be declared within the code. Build and run the code.

Type two different values separated by a space. As you can see, the code displays the larger of the two values. Now, let's talk about the limitations.

In the C language, a function can return only one value. You cannot return multiple values, nor can we think of a reason why you would want to. You can return an array or a structure variable from a function. These variable types are covered in a later chapter. But yet they remain single variables. We would like to explain the *main* function.

As you can see here in the previous source code, main is an integer function. The return statement is required, and an integer value must be specified. The parenthesis for the main function is empty. This is a shortcut—a cheat.

The compiler knows the arguments for the main function. Two of them exist, but you don't need to specify them if they don't get used. The parenthesis remains empty in the *main* function. This is not something, however, you can get away with other functions you declare and use.

CHARACTER MANIPULATION FUNCTIONS

So much goes on with characters that the C library offers a host of character manipulation functions. In this section, we introduce a few of those functions and show you how to use them in your code. As a bonus, we offer an introduction to logical expressions, which can also come into play when working with characters.

In your C code, characters appear either individually, or marching along in an array called a string. You can manipulate characters one at a time or, more commonly, in the string. The code below includes a ctype.h header file, which prototypes the character testing and manipulation functions:

```
1       #include <stdio.h>
2       #include <ctype.h>
3
4       int main()
5       {
6               int ch = 'a';
7
```

```
8              printf("Big %c\n",toupper(ch));
9              printf("Little %c\n",tolower(ch));
10             printf("What begins with %c?\n",ch);
11
12             return(0);
13    }
14
15
```

At lines 8 and 9, you see the *toupper* and *tolower* functions. The *toupper* function generates the uppercase version of a letter. The *tolower* function generates the lowercase version of a letter. The results are used immediately in the *printf* functions. Note that these functions require integer values, not characters. You can display the result by using %c in the *printf* function, even though they are integer variables. Build and run the code.

As you can see by the output of the final *printf* statement at line 10, the *toupper* and *tolower* functions did not affect the variable *ch*. They merely generate an upper or lowercase equivalent. You can use these functions on a string as well. To do that, you must dissect the string in a loop. Take a look at the code below:

```
1      #include <stdio.h>
2      #include <ctype.h>
3
4      int main()
5      {
6              int c;
```

```
7
8              do
9              {
10                     c = getchar();
11                     c = toupper(c);
12                     putchar(c);
13             }
14             while(c != '\n');
15
```

Again, an integer variable is used in the *toupper* function. Input is processed and converted to upper case at line 11, then output. You won't see the output until you press the Enter key because the C language is stream-oriented. Build and run the code.

Go ahead and type some text. Press the Enter key. The output is all caps, but note how the punctuation symbols and spaces are unaffected by the *toupper* function. Most of the functions defined in the ctype.h header file are testing functions. They are used to evaluate the type of character, such as whether it is a letter, number, space, or upper or lower case. These functions return true and false values, which you can use in your code to see what's been typed.

As an example, the code below uses the *isalpha* function to determine whether a character is a letter of the alphabet, or some other character.

```
1       #include <stdio.h>
2       #include <ctype.h>
```

```
3
4        int main()
5        {
6                int acter;
7
8                do
9                {
10                       acter = getchar();
11                       if(isalpha(acter))
12                               putchar(acter);
13               }
14               while( acter != '\n');
15
```

The function returns 'true' if it is or 'false' otherwise. In the do/while loop, input is received and checked. The *if* statement at line 11 returns true if the character is a letter of the alphabet. If so, it is displayed. Build and run the code. Type a bunch of text including symbols and numbers. Press the Enter key, and only the alphabet characters—both upper and lowercase—are displayed.

You can modify the source code to try out many of the character manipulation functions. For example, change *isalpha* in line 11 to *isupper*. Now, only the upper case letters are displayed. Save, build and run to test the change.

Other functions defined in the ctype.h header file include:
- islower – detects only lowercase letters
- isnumber – returns true for any number character 0 through 9

- isblank – detects whitespace characters—space tab or new line

You can also craft your own character manipulation functions, but it helps to know about C logical operators.

LOGICAL OPERATORS

The C language's logical operators are used to compare two or more expressions. The operators determine whether the result is true or false. Three operators are available to use:

- &&   logical AND
- || logical OR
- !   logical NOT

These are often written in all caps, so that they are not confused with the regular words. For an AND operation to be true, both conditions must be true—*this* AND *that*. For an OR operator, either of the conditions must be true—*this* OR *that*. And for the NOT operator, the condition must be false, which is backwards, but that's how NOT works—NOT *this*.

As an example, the AND operator evaluates two conditions below:

```
a = 7;
if( a > 0 && a , 10 )
```

```
TRUE && TRUE == TRUE
```

Here, both conditions are true. Therefore, the *if* statement is executed. In the example below, one of the conditions is false. Therefore, the *if* statements are skipped.

a = 7;
if(a > 0 && a < 5)

TRUE && FALSE == FALSE

In the logical OR operator, only one of the conditions need to be true. Below, the *if* statement would be executed.

a = 50;
if(a < 10 || a > 25)

FALSE || TRUE == TRUE

When both conditions are false, the if statement won't be executed.

a = 50;
if(a < 10 || a > 75)

FALSE || FALSE == FALSE

And in the case of NOT, it negates the condition. Here, both the conditions are false:

a = 50:
if(!(a!=50))

TRUE

Variable *a* is equal to *50*. However, the NOT operator turns that around and makes it true. Finally, in the C language, all values are considered true, except for zero, which is false. Typically, the value *1* is used for true. But it could also be negative 1 or any non-zero value. As an example of constructing your own character test, take a look at the code below:

```
1       #include <stdio.h>
2
3       int iscaps(int ch);
4
5       int main()
6       {
7               int c;
8
9               do
10              {
11                      c = getchar();
12                      if(iscaps(c));
13                              putchar(c);
14              }
15              while( c != '\n');
16
17              return(0);
18      }
19
20      int iscaps(int ch)
21      {
22              if( ch < 'A' || ch > 'Z')
```

```
23                      return(0);
24           else
25                      return(1);
26   }
27
28
```

A logical comparison is made at line 22. To understand how it works, read the condition: If the value of variable *ch* is less than *A* or the value of variable *ch* is greater than *Z*. When either of those conditions is false, meaning the character is not uppercase, the function returns false. Otherwise, the function returns true.

Suppose you wanted to change the *iscaps* function to *isLowerCase*, and have it return true or false based on that condition. How would you go about doing it? Well, the first thing to do is to change the name of the function to something more accurate.

```
1      #include <stdio.h>
2
3      int isLowerCase(int ch);
4
5      int main()
6      {
7              int c;
8
9              do
10             {
11                     c = getchar();
```

```
12                      if(isLowerCase(c));
13                          putchar(c);
14          }
15          while( c != '\n');
16
17          return(0);
18  }
19
20  int isLowerCase(int ch)
21  {
22          if( ch < 'a' || ch > 'z')
23                  return(0);
24      else
25                  return(1);
26  }
27
28
```

After changing the function calls appropriately, also change the 'A' to 'a', and 'Z' to 'z.' Save, build and run the code. As you can see in the output, only lowercase letters appear. You can create just about any character test by using logical operators. You'll see additional examples of using logical operators in the succeeding chapters of this book.

CHAPTER 9: WORKING WITH STRINGS

A string is a funny thing. It is not really a C language variable, but it is used that way. When it comes to manipulating strings in your code, you have to be really careful due to their unusual nature. This section discusses working with strings.

We'll show you how to gather information about a string, stick strings together, compare strings, and find one string inside another. These tasks represent the more popular string manipulation functions in the C language. Take a look at the code below:

```
1       #include <stdio.h>
2       #include <string.h>
3
4       int main()
5       {
6               char string[] = "Just how long am I?";
7               int len;
8
9               len = strlen(string);
10              printf("The following string:\n");
11              puts(string);
12              printf("is %d characters long.\n",len);
13
14              return(0);
15      }
16
17
```

STRLEN

A string is declared at line 6. It is a character array, so the *char* variable type is specified. The variable name is *string*, followed by empty brackets. The string length function *strlen* appears at line 9. It returns the number of characters in a string, which is stored in the *len* variable. Build and run the code.

The string is 19 characters long. You can also count the characters in the source code, but you won't always have the luxury of knowing the exact amount. For example, what if the user types in a string. Take a look at the code below:

```
1       #include <stdio.h>
2       #include <stdio.h>
3
4       int main()
5    {
6               char input[64];        /* 63 characters plus
null */
7               int len;
8
9               printf("Instructions: ");
10              fgets(input,64,stdin);
11              len = strlen(input);
12              printf("You typed %d characters of
instructions.\n",len);
13
14              return(0);
15   }
```

Input is fetched by using the *fgets* function, and then it is stored in an input buffer. Afterwards, the *strlen* function fetches the length of the string. The next statement displays the result. Build and run the code.

Keep in mind that strings in C end with a null character. Storage must be allocated for that extra character. The program generates the character, but you must provide room for it in the input buffer. The *strlen* function does not count that null character when it measures the string's length. Now take a look at the code example below:

```
1      #include <stdio.h>
2
3      int main()
4      {
5            char first[] = "I would like to go ";
6            char second[] = "from here to there\n";
7
8            return(0);
9      }
10
```

STRCAT / CONCATENATION

This is only partial code. We're going to figure out how to stick these two strings—*first* and *second*—together to make another new string. In many programming languages, the addition operator does the trick. For example, some programming languages might write the code this way to connect the two strings together to make a new string:

```
1      #include <stdio.h>
2
3      int main()
4      {
5              char first[] = "I would like to go ";
6              char second[] = "from here to there\n";
7
8              printf("%s\n", first+second);
9
10             return(0);
11     }
12
```

However, in the C programming language, this would not work. You could display both strings back to back, but that's not the solution we're after. What you need to do is to stick the strings together. Now, rather than say, "stick the strings together," C programmers say, "concatenate," which comes from the Latin word for sticking two strings together.

But before that, fix up the code. First, create a storage location, or a buffer, for the resulting two strings.

```
1      #include <stdio.h>
2
3      int main()
4      {
5              char first[] = "I would like to go ";
6              char second[] = "from here to there\n";
```

```
7          char storage[64];

7

8          printf("%s\n", first+second);

9

10         return(0);

11    }

12
```

As you can see at line 7, we've created a storage location—buffer—for the resulting two strings. You can set the storage buffer to accommodate any number of characters—including the null character. In our example here, we're just setting it to 64.

Next, we're going to copy the first string into that storage location. The *strcpy*, or *stringcopy* function copies one string into another. At line 9, the string *'first'* is duplicated into the storage buffer.

```
1          #include <stdio.h>

2

3          int main()

4          {

5                  char first[] = "I would like to go ";

6                  char second[] = "from here to there\n";

7                  char storage[64];

7

8                  strcpy(storage,first);

9

10                 return(0);

11         }

12
```

Also, you need to prototype that *strcpy* function. All string functions are declared in the string.h header file.

```
1       #include <stdio.h>
2       #include <string.h>
3
4       int main()
5       {
6               char first[] = "I would like to go ";
7               char second[] = "from here to there\n";
8               char storage[64];
9
10              strcpy(storage,first);
11
12              return(0);
13      }
14
```

Next, you need to stick the string 'second' into the end of the storage buffer. The *strcat*, or string concatenation statement tacks the string 'second' onto the end of whatever is inside the storage buffer—concatenation. Then finally, display the results.

```
1       #include <stdio.h>
2       #include <string.h>
3
4       int main()
5       {
6               char first[] = "I would like to go ";
```

```
7          char second[] = "from here to there\n";
8          char storage[64];
9
10         strcpy(storage,first);
11         strcat(storage,second);
12         printf("Here is your string:\n%s",storage);
12
13         return(0);
14    }
15
```

Save, build and run the code. As you can see in the output, it worked.

STRCMP / STRING COMPARE

Another popular string function compares two strings. The code below uses the *strcmp*, or string compare function to compare two strings:

```
1      #include <stdio.h>
2      #include <string.h>
3
4      int main()
5      {
6          char password[9];
7          int compare;
8
9          printf("Enter your password: ");
10         scanf("%8s",password);
```

```
11              compare = strcmp(password,"secret");
12              if( compare == 0 )
13                      puts("You have been granted
access!");
14              else
15                      puts("Intruder alert!");
16
17              return(0);
18      }
19
20
```

The value returned is zero when both strings are the same. This is one of those weird times when zero actually means true. Values less than or greater than zero indicate incorrect matches. You'll also notice that the *scanf* function limits input only up to eight characters. The input matches the eight character limitation on the buffer. The buffer is nine characters to account for the null character at the end of the string. Build and run the code.

Now, try a few passwords before you try the real one, which is "*secret*." Also, this code doesn't need the compare variable. You can remove it. Delete it twice from the code and replace it with a function directly. Place the strcmp function inside of the if statement like so:

```
1       #include <stdio.h>
2       #include <string.h>
3
```

```
4       int main()
5       {
6               char password[9];

7

8               printf("Enter your password: ");
9               scanf("%8s",password);
10              if( strcmp(password,"secret") == 0 )
11                      puts("You have been granted
access!");
12              else
13                      puts("Intruder alert!");

14

15              return(0);
16      }
```

STRSTR/ STRING STRING

The final string function we'd like to show is called *strstr*, or string string. It is used to find one string inside of another. Take a look at the code below:

```
1       #include <stdio.h>
2       #include <string.h>

3

4       int main()
5       {
6               char source_string[] = "I am a stranger in a
strange land";
7               char find_me[] = "strange";

8
```

```
9              if( strstr(source_string,find_me) == NULL)
10                  puts("String not found!");
11          else
12                  printf("Founc '%s' in
'%s'\n",find_me,source_string);
13
14              return(0);
15      }
16
17
```

This code uses the *strstr* function. It is a little weird because you really need to know a little more about pointers to effectively use this function. That knowledge is gleaned in a later chapter. But for now, the *strstr* function is included as part of the *if* statement at line 9.

It returns a pointer, or the location of the string *find_me* in the string *source_string*. If no match is made, then the value NULL is returned. Again, NULL is a pointer thing. Build and run the code. As you can see from the output, the string is found.

You can alter the text for the string *find_me* to prove that the function actually works. Until you've reached the rocky shoals of pointer land, that's about the best that can be done with the *strstr* function.

CHAPTER 10: C LANGUAGE CONSTANTS

Occasionally, when learning something new, you need to pause and reflect. That's the topic of this section: pausing and reflecting specifically, with regards to variables and values. We'll also introduce a few new concepts—things we feel it's about time you knew, especially if you're new to learning the C programming language. In this section we cover creating and using constants. Plus, we'll also discuss some of the *printf* function's placeholders.

A constant in the C language is different from an immediate value and a variable. It is more like a universal value that doesn't change throughout the code. Constants are values used consistently throughout your source code.

There are things that do not change. They are created by the preprocessor #define directive. Normally the constant is written in all caps, one word, or with underlines only. Now when the compiler encounters a constant, it expands it out to its assigned value.

In the example below, the constant *version* is created and it is assigned to the value 3. The compiler converts the word version into the immediate value 3 throughout the code.

#define VERSION 3

- Constant is named VERSION
- Has a value of 3
- Does not end with a semi-colon

Remember, preprocessor directives are not C language statements. Do not put a semi-colon after the assignment, unless you need the semi-colon to be a part of whatever is being defined, which hardly ever happens. Just don't add a semi-colon.

Below is a string constant defined as *AUTHOR*. The string must be enclosed in double quotes. This is an example of one constant that uses two other constants to calculate its value.

#define AUTHOR "Adolf Hitler"

- The constant is named AUTHOR
- The value is the string "Adolf Hitler."
- No semi-colon is used.

Below, the constant *GAME_GRID* would equal *120*, unless either the *ROWS* or *COLUMNS* constants are changed. They wouldn't be changed in the code. They would be changed in the define statement that you see below:

#define ROWS 20
#define COLUMNS 60
#define GAME_GRID ROWS*COLUMNS

- Three constants are created: ROWS, COLUMNS, and GAME_GRID
- The value of GAME_GRID is based on the product of constants ROWS and COLUMNS.

Take a look at the code below:

This code is based on the previous example that we've used in an earlier chapter. We've cleaned it up a bit and we've set up some constants in the code, specifically two #define directives to set the numbers of rows and columns in a grid.

```
1       #include <stdio.h>
2       #include <stdlib.h>
3       #include <time.h>
4
5       #define ROWS 10
6       #define COLUMNS 10
7
8       int main()
9       {
10              int row, column;
11
12              srand((unsigned)time(NULL));
13
14              for(row=0;row<10;row++)
15              {
16
for(column=0;column<10;column++)
17                              printf("%2d\t",rand() % 100);
18                      putchar('\n');
19              }
20
21              return(0);
22      }
23
24
```

Now, let's change the value 10—used as an immediate value in the loops—to reflect the constants.

```
1       #include <stdio.h>
2       #include <stdlib.h>
3       #include <time.h>
4
5       #define ROWS 10
6       #define COLUMNS 10
7
8       int main()
9       {
10              int row, column;
11
12              srand((unsigned)time(NULL));
13
14              for(row=0;row<ROWS;row++)
15              {
16
for(column=0;column<COLUMNS;column++)
17                          printf("%2d\t",rand() % 100);
18                  putchar('\n');
19              }
20
21              return(0);
22      }
23
24
```

Save the changes, and then build and run the code. The program still outputs 100 random numbers in ten rows and ten columns. But now you can easily change that to say twenty rows of seven columns. All you need to do to make that change is to change the constants.

```
1       #include <stdio.h>
2       #include <stdlib.h>
3       #include <time.h>
4
5       #define ROWS 20
6       #define COLUMNS 7
7
8       int main()
9       {
10              int row, column;
11
12              srand((unsigned)time(NULL));
13
14              for(row=0;row<ROWS;row++)
15              {
16
for(column=0;column<COLUMNS;column++)
17                              printf("%2d\t",rand() % 100);
18                      putchar('\n');
19              }
20
21              return(0);
22      }
23
24
```

You do not have to hunt through the code to find those proper values. That is how constants can save you time. Save, build and run the code. As you can see from the output, you now have seven columns of twenty rows. Another example of using constants can be seen in the sample code below:

```
1       #include <stdio.h>

2

3       #define INPUT_MAX 64

4

5       int main()

6       {

7               char input[INPUT_MAX];

8

9               printf("Instructions: ");

10              fgets(input,INPUT_MAX,stdin);

11              puts("Thank you! Here are your
instructions:");

12              puts(input);

13

14              return(0);

15      }

16

17
```

This code is an update to an example from an earlier chapter. The number of characters to be input is set by the *INPUT_MAX* constant defined at line 3. The constant is then used to set the buffer size at line 7, and again with the fgets function at line 10.

The advantage here is that you can change both values at once simply by modifying the *INPUT_MAX* constant. You do not have to hunt through the code. Now take a look at the code below:

```
1      #include <stdio.h>
2
3      int main()
4      {
5              float a;
6              float b = 5.0;
7
8              printf("Input a number: ");
9              scanf("%f",&a);
10             printf("%f / %f = %f\n",a,b,a/b);
11
12             return(0);
13     }
14
15
```

This is also a modification to an earlier example used in an earlier chapter. Build and run the code to help you remember what the problem was. You can fix this problem by adjusting the placeholders in the *printf* statement. Modify each %f placeholder at line 10 by inserting .1 inside each one so that they read:

```
1      #include <stdio.h>
2
3      int main()
```

```
4       {
5               float a;
6               float b = 5.0;
7
8               printf("Input a number: ");
9               scanf("%f",&a);
10              printf("%.1f / %.1f = %.1f\n",a,b,a/b);
11
12              return(0);
13      }
14
15
```

Save the changes, and then build and run the code. The .1 format limits floating point output to only one digit after the decimal point. Edit it again and type .3 for the format in the *printf* statement.

```
1       #include <stdio.h>
2
3       int main()
4       {
5               float a;
6               float b = 5.0;
7
8               printf("Input a number: ");
9               scanf("%f",&a);
10              printf("%.3f / %.3f = %.3f\n",a,b,a/b);
11
12              return(0);
```

```
13      }
14
15
```

Save, build and run the code. Now, three digits appear after the decimal point. Now let's return again to our previous CONSTANT example:

```
1       #include <stdio.h>
2       #include <stdlib.h>
3       #include <time.h>
4
5       #define ROWS 20
6       #define COLUMNS 7
7
8       int main()
9       {
10              int row, column;
11
12              srand((unsigned)time(NULL));
13
14              for(row=0;row<ROWS;row++)
15              {
16
for(column=0;column<COLUMNS;column++)
17                      printf("%2d\t",rand() % 100);
18                  putchar('\n');
19              }
20
```

```
21              return(0);
22      }
23
24
```

At line 17, you see at *2* between the *percent* and letter '*d*.' What the *2* does is set an output width to two characters minimum. When a single digit appears in the output, they'll write a line. Build and run the code. See how singular digits are lined up in the output.

Now edit the code again and remove the *2*. Save, build and run the code. Now, the single digits do not look right. No one expects them to line up in the tens column. The placeholders have lots of options. These can be sandwiched between the percent sign and their letter. We could dedicate thousands of chapters to write them all, but another one to look at is %s found in the code below:

```
1       #include <stdio.h>
2
3       int main()
4       {
5               char right[] = "right";
6               char left[] = "left";
7
8               printf("%20s\n",right);
9               printf("%-20s\n",left);
10
11              return(0);
12      }
13
14
```

The two strings, RIGHT and LEFT, are displayed by using %s placeholders. But there are extra characters between the percent and the s. The *20* specifies an output width, just like the *2* in between %d in the previous example.

In line 8, the %20s right justifies the output—adjusting the string's location based on its length inside that width. In line 9, the negative sign before the 20 left justifies the string, which is how text is normally displayed. Build and run this code to see how it works.

The width argument in the %s placeholder, sets the width to twenty characters. This placeholder is ideal for displaying lists and tables. Many more placeholder width, precision, padding, and other options are available. The documentation for the printf function lists the variety, plus a few examples.

CHAPTER 11: C LANGUAGE ARRAYS

An array is simply a collection of more than one of the same type of variable. For example, a list of high scores is a type of array, as would be how many miles you run per day, even if that list contains lots of zeros. Of course, strings in the C language are an array of single character variables.

In this section, we introduce the concept of an array. You'll see how to create an array, how to fill it with data, how to access that data, and we'll also divulge some secrets about character arrays also known as strings. Below, you see the way NOT to do multiple values in your code—four separate float variables are created and filled with data:

```
1        #include <stdio.h>
2
3        int main()
4        {
5
6
7                temp1 = 84.9;
8                temp2 = 83.7;
9                temp3 = 85.8;
10               temp4 = 88.2;
11
12               printf("Local temperatures:\n");
13               printf("Station 1: %.1f\n",temp1);
```

```
14              printf("Station 2: %.1f\n",temp2);
15              printf("Station 3: %.1f\n",temp3);
16              printf("Station 4: %.1f\n",temp4);
17
18              return(0);
19
20      }
21
22
```

They are then displayed using four separate *printf* statements. Each variable requires its own repetitive statement. You can build and run this code, but why bother. Instead, we'll show you a better way to deal with multiple variables of the same type. That way is the array. Take a look at the code below:

```
1       #include <stdio.h>
2
3       int main()
4       {
5               float temps[4] = { 84.9, 83.7, 85.8, 88.2 };
6               int x;
7
8               printf("Local temperatures:\n");
9               for(x=0;x<4;x++)
10                      printf("Station %d:
%.1f\n",x,temps[x]);
11
12              return(0);
```

```
13     }
14
15
```

This is the array version of the previous example. The array *temps* is created at line 5. It contains four elements, and each element is assigned in the brackets that follow. The loop at line 9   displays all four element's values by using a single *printf* function.

ANATOMY OF AN ARRAY

An array is simply a collection of multiple variables—all of the same type. It has a declaration similar to any other variable, but with square brackets after the variable name. The brackets hold the number of elements in the array. They can be blank if the elements are specified when the array is declared. Below, the integer array DELIVERIES has room for fifteen elements.

int deliveries[15];

Integer array TOTALS has three elements, which are assigned in curly brackets.

int totals[] = { 5, 13, 6 };

The final element does not have a comma. If you put a comma there, the compiler believes that you have forgotten something. You can also list array elements on a line by themselves. Except for the final element, don't forget to put the commas. Remember to close the curly bracket and add a semi-colon.

Each element in the array is its own variable. You specify the element between the square brackets. The first element is element *zero*. You can also use an integer variable to specify array elements. Below, variable *n* represents a specific element in the totals array:

printf("%d\n",totals[n]);

The element is used like any other variable. It can find itself inside a printf function, or it can be used with an assignment operator as shown below:

totals[n] = 14;

You cannot change the number of elements in an array after the array has been declared. Some tricks exist to work around this limitation. But for now, just accept it as a rule. Also, don't forget that the first element in an array is *zero*, not *1*.

Humans start counting at *1*, the C language starts counting at *0*. An integer array CALORIES is declared at line 7 in the code below:

```
1       #include <stdio.h>
2
3       #define MEALS 3
4
5       int main()
6       {
7               int calories[MEALS];
8               int x,total;
```

```
9
10              total = 0;
11              puts("Calorie Counter");
12              for(x=0;x<MEALS;x++)
13              {
14                      printf("Calories at meal %d: ",x+1);
15                      scanf("%d",&calories[x]);
16                      total = total +calories[x];
17              }
18              printf("You had a total of %d
calories.\n",total);
19
20              return(0);
21      }
22
23
```

It has the MEALS element and the MEALS constant is set to 3 at line 3. A *for* loop at line 12 reads in three values. See how the *for* loop starts at *zero*. That comes in handy when working with arrays as the first element is *zero*.

In line 14, however, *1* is added to the looping variable *x*, which makes the numbers more accommodating to humans running the program. The *scanf* statement at line 15 reads the values into each array element. An array element is an individual variable, so the ampersand is required.

At line 16, the value input is added to the total variable. Now build and run the code. Type in some easy numbers to confirm the computer's math. You'll see the variable *total* is initialized at line 10. That is required. Otherwise, the variable may contain garbage. In C, variables are not initialized until they are assigned a value.

Comment out line 10 to prove this. Save, build and run the code to see if it has any effect. Of course, the number is off because the *total* variable is not properly initialized. There's an off chance that it may be correct because a random number could be *zero*, in which case 600 would show up.

Strings are character arrays. Normally, they are declared by using double quotes. Take a look at the code below:

```
1       #include <stdio.h>
2
3       int main()
4       {
5               char text[] = "I am a string!";
6
7               puts(text);
8
9               return(0);
10      }
11
12
```

The character array TEXT is declared at line 5. This is really simple, and is one of the best ways to declare a string or a character array.

Now take a look at the code below:

```
1       #include <stdio.h>
2
3       int main()
4       {
5               char text[] = {
6                       'I', ' ', 'a', 'm', ' ', 'a', ' ',
7                       's', 't', 'r', 'i', 'n', 'g', '!', '\0'
8               };
9
10              puts(text);
11
12              return(0);
13      }
14
15
```

This code works the same as the previous exercise, but the character array is declared character-by-character, which is a phenomenal waste of time. Build and run the code. It works, but it is just too much effort.

The code does, however, point out the final character in all C language strings that must be specified: the null character. It is shown in the previous code as the escape sequence '\0.' When you use double quotes to declare a string, the compiler automatically adds the *null* for you. But when you specify one character at a time, you must remember to add the *null*.

The *null* comes in handy when you display a string one character at a time. Take a look at the code below:

```
1       #include <stdio.h>
2
3       int main()
4       {
5               char hello[] = "Greetings, human!\n";
6               int n;
7
8               n = 0;
9               while( hello[n] != '\0')
10              {
11                      putchar(hello[n]);
12                      n++;
13              }
14
15              return(0);
16      }
17
18
```

This code displays the string in the *hello* array one character at a time. The while loop marches through the string until the null character is encountered. It spits out single characters by incrementing variable *n* as it progresses. Build and run the code.

Because the null character evaluates to the false condition in the C language, you can shorten the *while* decision to this:

185

```
1       #include <stdio.h>

2

3       int main()

4       {

5               char hello[] = "Greetings, human!\n";

6               int n;

7

8               n = 0;

9               while( hello[n] )

10              {

11                      putchar(hello[n]);

12                      n++;

13              }

14

15              return(0);

16      }

17

18
```

Make that change to your code, and then save, build and run it. As you can see, the same output is generated, although the source code is a tad less readable to a beginning programmer. The typical array in the C language is simply a series of variables—all of the same type marching off together. But not every type of data is a single line. Sometimes you have to deal with a grid. In that case, you enter into the realm of the multi-dimensional array.

MULTI-DIMENSIONAL ARRAYS

This section uncovers the mystery of the multi-dimensional array. You'll learn how to configure such an array and access its values. You'll also see how multi-dimensional arrays apply to strings. To visualize a multi-dimensional array, think of a grid—you have rows and columns. Take a look at the code below:

```
1       #include <stdio.h>
2
3       #define ROWS 4
4       #define COLUMNS 4
5
6       int main()
7       {
8               int grid[ROWS] [COLUMNS];
9               int x,y;
10
11              /* initialize the array */
12              f0r(x=0;x<ROWS;x++)
13                      for(y=0;y<COLUMNS;y++)
14                              grid[x] [y] = 0;
15
16              /* display the grid */
17              for(x=0;x<ROWS;x++)
18              {
19                      for(y=0;y<COLUMNS;y++)
20                              printf("%d.%d: %d\t",x,y,grid[x] [y]);
21                      putchar('\n');
```

```
22               }

23

24               return(0);
```

The array is declared at line 8. Two sets of square brackets are used—one for each dimension in the array. So *grid* is an integer array. It is effectively a 2 dimensional array. Lines 12 through 14 use a nested loop to fill each array element, with the value zero initializing the array.

In line 14, you see that individual array elements require two square brackets as reference. Again, think of each as rows and columns. Then, the nested loops starting at line 17 print the array in rows and columns. Build and run the code.

The output shows each array element as it would be referenced. The first one is element '0.0.' That is the first element in both directions. As a thought experiment, how would you modify the code to set the value of the third element in both dimensions to the value *1*.

We hope you remember that arrays start with element *zero*. The third element is actually referenced as grid '2.2.' We're going to add a line that reads 'grid 2.2 = 1.'

```
1       #include <stdio.h>

2

3       #define ROWS 4

4       #define COLUMNS 4

5
```

```
6        int main()
7        {
8                int grid[ROWS] [COLUMNS];
9                int x,y;
10
11               /* initialize the array */
12               f0r(x=0;x<ROWS;x++)
13                       for(y=0;y<COLUMNS;y++)
14                               grid[x] [y] = 0;
15
16               grid[2] [2] = 1;
17               /* display the grid */
18               for(x=0;x<ROWS;x++)
19               {
20                       for(y=0;y<COLUMNS;y++)
21                               printf("%d.%d:
%d\t",x,y,grid[x] [y]);
22                       putchar('\n');
23               }
24
25               return(0);
```

Save that change, and then build and run the code. This is how the value looks with the value 1 at grid 2.2. You can also conjure up a two-dimensional character array, as is shown in the code below:

```
1        #include <stdio.h>
2
3        int main()
```

```
4       {
5               char names[4] [7] = {
6                       "Mickey",
7                       "Minnie",
8                       "Goofy",
9                       "Pluto",
10              };
11              int x;
12
13              for(x=0;x<4;x++)
14                      printf("%s\n",names[x]);
15
16              return(0);
17      }
18
19
```

A two-dimensional character array is simply a collection of strings, but with one important caveat: The array must be dimensioned to handle the largest string. Remember, a two-dimensional array is a grid. Here, the longest string is six letters long, plus one element for the *null* character. That makes seven elements for each string.

When printing strings from a two-dimensional character array, you need only specify the first dimension, which is done on line 14. Build and run the code. The C language also offers three-dimensional arrays, and even more dimensions than that. When you create such an array, you need one set of brackets for each dimension. Things can get pretty complex in a hurry. For now, concentrate on playing with two-dimensional arrays.

As a thought, whether you believe it or not, if you've been reading this book from the beginning, you have everything you need to know to program a rudimentary Tick-Tack-Toe computer game. Give it a try.

CHAPTER 12: C LANGUAGE STRUCTURES

Another variable type in the C language is the structure. It is actually a combination of existing variable types all tied together into a single unit. A structure variable simply has many parts like a record in a database. This chapter presents the concept of the structure. You'll see how to set up a structure, create structure variables, and how to access structure members.

We'll discuss how to fill data into a structure, as well as the interesting idea of placing one structure inside another. The code below is not a complete code, of course, but shows you how a structure can be created in the C language.

```
1       #include <stdio.h>

2

3       int main()

4       {

5               struct record {

6                       int account;

7                       float balance;

8               };

9

10              return(0);

11      }

12

13
```

The keyword *struct* is followed by the name of the structure. In this case, the name is *'record'*. The structure members are contained in curly brackets; each ending with a semi-colon because the whole deal is a statement. The structure members are variable declarations. Inside this structure, you'll find an *int* and a *float* member. The *int* member is named *'account'*. The *float* member is named *'balance'*.

By itself, the structured declaration merely creates a type of structure, like a new type of variable in the code. To use the structure, you need to declare a variable of the structure type. On line 9 we're going to type the following:

```
1       #include <stdio.h>
2
3       int main()
4       {
5               struct record {
6                       int account;
7                       float balance;
8               };
9               struct record my_bank;
10
11              return(0);
12      }
13
14
```

This statement creates a variable named *my_bank* of the *record* structure type. To access the structure's members, you need to reference both the variable name, as well as the member name. Let's add two new lines. The structure variable name comes first, then a dot, then the member name. They must be assigned values equal to the variable type. In this case, an integer and a floating point value.

```
1      #include <stdio.h>
2
3      int main()
4        {
5              struct record {
6                    int account;
7                    float balance;
8              };
9              struct record my_bank;
10
11             my_bank.account = 123456;
12             my_bank.balance = 6543.21;
13
14             return(0);
15       }
16
17
```

Save these changes, and then build and run the code. To create another record structure variable called *your_bank*, you simply have to echo the existing statements. You can also fill the members in that structure simply by copying the previous statements and replacing '*my_bank*' with '*your_bank*.'

```
1       #include <stdio.h>
2
3       int main()
4       {
5               struct record {
6                       int account;
7                       float balance;
8               };
9               struct record my_bank;
10              struct record your_bank;
11
12              my_bank.account = 123456;
13              my_bank.balance = 6543.21;
14              print("In account %d I have
%.2f\n",my_bank.account,my_bank.balance)
15
16              return(0);
17      }
18
19
```

You could also preset the information inside the structure. Take a look at the code below:

```
1       #include <stdio.h>
2
3       int main()
4       {
5               struct person {
```

```
6                       char name[32];
7                       int age;
8          };
9          struct person president = {
10                      "George Washington",
11                      67
12         };
13
14         printf("%s was %d years
old\n",president.name,president.age);
15
16         return(0);
17  }
18
19
```

In this code, a structure named *person* is declared. A variable of the person type is declared at line 9. It is named *'president'*. The president structure variable is immediately assigned with values. The values match the structure member types and are enclosed in curly brackets. Run this code to ensure that it works.

One thing to note in the structure is how you assign a string to a structure member. Take a look at the code below:

```
1      #include <stdio.h>
2
3      int main()
4          {
```

```
5          struct person {
6                  char name[32];
7                  int age;
8              };
9          struct person president;
10
11         president.name = "George Washington";
12         president.age = 67;
13
14         printf("%s was %d years
old\n",president.name,president.age);
15
16             return(0);
17     }
18
19
```

If you can see what's wrong, great. Otherwise, build the code and then check the build log to see the specific error. As you can see, it is incompatible. You cannot use the assignment operator with a string. That is because strings are not variables. They are arrays. Here's how to solve it:

```
1      #include <stdio.h>
2      #include <string.h>
3
4      int main()
5      {
6              struct person {
```

```
7            char name[32];
8            int age;
9         };
10        struct person president;
11
12        strcpy(president.name,"George
Washington");
13        president.age = 67;
14
15        printf("%s was %d years
old\n",president.name,president.age);
16
17        return(0);
18    }
19
20
```

Now, it works. You can insert any variable type into a C language structure—even another structure. Take a look at the code below:

```
1     #include <stdio.h>
2     #include <string.h>
3
4     int main()
5     {
6            struct date {
7                   int year;
8                   int month;
9                   int day;
```

```
10              };
11              struct person {
12                      char name[32];
13                      struct date birthday;
14              };
15              struct person friend;
16
17              strcpy(friend.name,"Anita Mann");
18              friend.birthday.year = 1975;
19              friend.birthday.month = 6;
20              friend.birthday.day = 1;
21
22              printf("My friend %s was born on
%d/%d/%d\n",
23                      friend.name,
24                      friend.birthday.month,
25                      friend.birthday.day,
26                      friend.birthday.year);
27
28              return(0);
29      }
30
```

In this code, you see definitions for two structures. The first, *date*, is defined at line 6. It holds members year, month, and day. The second structure, *person*, is declared at line 11. It contains a name array, but also the date structure in the form of a *birthday* variable.

A person variable structure *friend* is declared at line 15. Lines 17 through 20 build a friend variable and *strcpy* is used to assign the string. For the structure member birthday, note how two dots are used to fill in the substructure members in lines 18, 19, and 20. That's how it works. That is how structures within structures are referenced. Build and run this code.

By the way, most programmers will declare a structure and then create a structure variable in the same statement. You can do that here at line 14. Specify the variable name friend at the end of line 14, then remove line 15.

```
1       #include <stdio.h>
2       #include <string.h>
3
4       int main()
5       {
6               struct date {
7                       int year;
8                       int month;
9                       int day;
10              };
11              struct person {
12                      char name[32];
13                      struct date birthday;
14              } friend;
15
16              strcpy(friend.name,"Anita Mann");
17              friend.birthday.year = 1975;
18              friend.birthday.month = 6;
```

```
19              friend.birthday.day = 1;
20
21              printf("My friend %s was born on
%d/%d/%d\n",
22                  friend.name,
23                  friend.birthday.month,
24                  friend.birthday.day,
25                  friend.birthday.year);
26
27              return(0);
28      }
29
30
```

Save the changes, and then build and run the code. The output is the same. It is preferred not to use this shortcut when coding in C because it makes the code less readable. But you're free to use it, and you'll see it quite frequently in other C codes.

CHAPTER 13: C LANGUAGE TIME FUNCTIONS

We've yet to encounter a programmable device that didn't have some sort of internal clock. The computer has a clock, and thanks to the Internet, modern computers keep accurate track of the time. When your code needs to access that information, you dip into the C language library's assortment of time functions.

In this chapter, you'll see how time functions work in the C language. You'll learn how to check the time, read time values, and how to gather information about the current date. The code below uses the direct value generated by the time function, as shown by the second argument in the *printf* function at line 6:

```
1       #include <stdio.h>
2       #include <time.h>
3
4       int main()
5       {
6               printf("The current time is
%ld\n",time(NULL));
7
8               return(0);
9       }
10
11
```

You'll see that the placeholder is '%ld," which is a long integer value, or a very large integer. That's the type of value returned from the time function. The time function itself requires an argument. In our example, we're using the NULL pointer constant to keep the function happy. Also keeping the compiler happy is the inclusion of the time.h header file at line 2. Build and run this code.

It is actually what's referred to as the Unix Epoch time, or the number of seconds that have elapsed since January 1st 1970. To be relevant to a human being, the number is going to need some work. Normally, the value returned from the time function is saved. It is a long integer value, but the variable type is known as 'time_t.'

Insert a new line in the code to declare variable *now* as a *time_t* type. To assign a value to the *now* variable, you must specify it as an argument in the time function. Yes, that's backwards. But several functions operate that way, including *scanf*. Like *scanf*, you must prefix the variable with an ampersand. Change the printf statement, so that the variable *now* appears as the second argument.

```
1       #include <stdio.h>
2       #include <time.h>
3
4       int main()
5       {
6               time_t (&now);
7
8               time(&now);
6               printf("The current time is %ld\n",now);
7
```

```
8              return(0);
9       }
10
11
```

Save these changes, and then build and run the code. The time is still shown as a big number, but it also shows that you have time left to complete this chapter. Moving along, the C library comes with a function that translates *time_t* values into strings. It is called the *ctime* function.

Edit the *printf* function in the previous code so that the second argument is now &ctime. Change the %ld placeholder to %s. This needs to be done because the *ctime* function generates a string.

```
1       #include <stdio.h>
2       #include <time.h>
3
4       int main()
5       {
6              time_t now;
7
8              time(&now);
6              printf("The current time is
%s\n",ctime(&now));
7
8              return(0);
9       }
10
11
```

Save, build and run the code. What you see is the current date and time. Unless you're reading this chapter right now, you'll see a different time. If you want to fetch specific time values, then you need to use the local time function. This function returns the address of a structure that holds individual time values such as the day, month, week, hour, and so forth. Take a look at the code below:

```
1       #include <stdio.h>
2       #include <time.h>
3
4       int main()
5       {
6               time_t now;
7               struct tm *right_now;
8
9               time(&now);
10              right_now = localtime(&now);
11              printf("Today is %d/%d at %d:%d\n",
12                      right_now->tm_mon,
13                      right_now->tm_mday,
14                      right_now->tm_hour,
15                      right_now->tm_min );
16
17              return(0);
18      }
19
20
```

The local time function at line 10 fills a structure with interesting information about the current time. The structure is declared at line 7. It is a pointer variable, which you'll learn about in a later chapter. The local function uses the current time value obtained at line 9. This fills the structure 'right_now.'

Some of that information available in the structure is displayed in the *printf* statement starting at line 11. We've split up the arguments on separate lines to make them more readable. But lines 12 to 15 are really a single statement. The C language does not let any extra spaces in there bother it. Four values are accessed from the *right_now* structure: the month, the day of the month, the hour, and minutes. These are all members of the *right_now* structure.

You see that the period structure member operator isn't used here. The ' -> ' is the member operator used for structure pointer variables. Build and run the code. Now you may notice that the month value is off. That is because C starts counting at *zero*, and the first month of the year—January—is month *zero*.

You can fix this code by adding *1* to the value return from the *right_now* structure. Other adjustments can be made as well. For example, if the current time is less than 10 minutes after the hour, then it appears as a single digit. Fix that by adding '*02*' to the %d placeholder. This argument increases the output width of the integer to two places. Plus it'll prefix a *zero* when the output is only one digit long.

```c
1       #include <stdio.h>
2       #include <time.h>
3
4       int main()
5       {
6               time_t now;
7               struct tm *right_now;
8
9               time(&now);
10              right_now = localtime(&now);
11              printf("Today is %d/%d at %d:%02d\n",
12                      right_now->tm_mon+1,
13                      right_now->tm_mday,
14                      right_now->tm_hour,
15                      right_now->tm_min );
16
17              return(0);
18      }
19
20
```

Save the changes, and then build and run the code.

CHAPTER 14: C LANGUAGE VARIABLES

A variable is a container for some type of data. In the C language, that container holds an integer, floating point character or other value. But philosophically speaking, what actually is a variable? In this chapter, we help you explore the concept of the variable. You'll see various ways a variable is described, how to determine its size, and its storage location.

In the typical C language variable declaration, you learned two tidbits about the variable: its type and its name. Below, you see an integer variable declared:

```
1       #include <stdio.h>

2

3       int main()

4       {

5               int a;

6

7               printf("The value of a is %d\n",a);

8

9               return(0);

10      }

11

12
```

It is an integer variable *int*, and its name is *a*. The variable is uninitialized, or never assigned a value. Even so, you can use it in the code, as is shown in line 7. Build and run this program. On your end, you might see any random value. Unlike other programming languages, C does not initialize variables as they are declared. Internally, the program allocates a chunk of memory to store the variable's information.

That chunk isn't initialized, and is not set to zero. It is just some location in the memory. Whatever value that's already there, is immediately absorbed by your variable as shown in whatever your output would be. The moral of the story is to always initialize variables before you use them. You can fix the previous code by adding a line like so:

```
1       #include <stdio.h>
2
3       int main()
4       {
5               int a;
6
7               a = 65;
8               printf("The value of a is %d\n",a);
9
10              return(0);
11      }
12
13
```

Save the changes, and then build and run the program. Now, the output is predictable. You also know something else about the variable: its value. Two additional tidbits about the variable can be obtained by using special C language operators. The first is the *sizeof* operator.

Sizeof is a keyword, but it is considered an operator. What it does is to return how many bytes of storage are used by a specific variable. That information may seem trivial, but it does come into play often in the C language. Take a look at the code below:

```
1       #include <stdio.h>

2

3       int main()

4       {

5               int a;

6

7               printf("An int variable occupies %lu bytes of
storage\n",sizeof(a));

8

9               return(0);

10      }

11

12
```

Variable *a* is not initialized here. But that's not an issue because it is not used. The *sizeof* operator is used in the *printf* statement. The *sizeof* operator simply evaluates variable *a* as an *int* variable to return the storage space it occupies. The *sizeof* operator returns a long, unassigned integer value. The placeholder required for that value is %lu. Build and run the code.

On this system, an integer occupies 4 bytes of storage. That's typical today. But 20 years ago, an integer only used 2 bytes of storage. Change *int* to *char* in the code at line 5, and at line 7 in the *printf* function. Save, build and run the code.

```
1       #include <stdio.h>
2
3       int main()
4       {
5               char a;
6
7               printf("A char variable occupies %lu bytes of
storage\n",sizeof(a));
8
9               return(0);
10      }
11
12
```

A character occupies only 1 byte of storage. Now, change to *float* and see how big that variable type is.

```
1       #include <stdio.h>
2
3       int main()
4       {
5               float a;
6
7               printf("A float variable occupies %lu bytes of
```

storage\n",sizeof(a));

8

9   return(0);

10   }

11

12

Save, build and run the code. On this system, a floating point variable occupies 4 bytes of storage. A long integer, or long *int* value, is designed to store really huge integers. To see how big it is, change *float* to *long* in the code.

```
1       #include <stdio.h>

2

3       int main()

4       {

5               long a;

6

7               printf("A long variable occupies %lu bytes of
storage\n",sizeof(a));

8

9               return(0);

10      }

11

12
```

Save, build and run the code. On this system, a long integer occupies 4 bytes of storage, which is the same for a regular integer. But on some systems, you may actually see 8 bytes of storage used for a long integer value. Likewise, a *double* value has twice the precision of a float. Change *long* to *double* in the code.

```
1       #include <stdio.h>
2
3       int main()
4       {
5               double a;
6
7               printf("A double variable occupies %lu bytes
of storage\n",sizeof(a));
8
9               return(0);
10      }
11
12
```

Save, build and run the code. Here, you actually see the double integer occupies 8 bytes of storage. By the way, you don't need to change the placeholder for any of these re-declarations. That's because the *sizeof* operator is what returns the long, unsigned integer value, not the variable itself.

Other information you can gather about a variable, includes its memory location. That tells you specifically where the variable's data—that 1, 4, or 8 bytes of storage—is located. To fetch a variable's memory location, use the ampersand operator.

You've already seen this operator used in the *scanf* and *timef* functions in the previous chapters. Take a look at the code below:

```
1       #include <stdio.h>
2
3       int main()
4       {
5               int a;
6               char b;
7               float c;
8
9               puts("Memory location:");
10              printf("A is at %p\n",&a);
11              printf("B is at %p\n",&b);
12              printf("C is at %p\n",&c);
13
14              return(0);
15      }
16
17
```

Three variables are declared in this code: an integer, a character, and a floating point value. These variables are not initialized because they are not used. But the program does allocate space for them at various locations in memory. To access those locations, the ampersand is prefixed to the variable name. To display the address, use the %p placeholder in the *printf* statement as show at lines 10, 11, and 12. Build and run this code.

The address output values will differ from machine to machine. Even their format will appear differently on different computers and different operating systems. At this point, the information may seem trivial. But it does play a major role when it comes to pointers, which are perhaps the scariest and most dreaded thing in all of the C language.

There are many C programmers who spend their careers artfully avoiding pointers, which are possible, but not smart.

CHAPTER 15: C LANGUAGE POINTERS

Pointers are puzzling. Yet, we hope this section clears the air for you. We'll discuss what a pointer is and how it is used. We promise to move nice and slow because this topic is a very important part of learning the C language.

The worst thing about pointers is their name. Pointers. It is descriptive, but a poor choice because you end up explaining a pointer by saying, "A pointer, points." That's pointless. But we can't change the name, so allow us to explain a pointer by giving you this definition: A pointer is a variable that holds a memory location—an address.

It is not just any address. You can't say, for example, "Let's see what's at memory location 96." Pointers do not work that way. The address must be the location of another variable. Pointer variables are declared similarly to other variables, although the variable name is prefixed by the pointer operator asterisk ' * '.

The pointer variable type matches the type of variable it references. For example, an *int* variable requires an *int* pointer. Pointer variables must be initialized before they are used. This is true of all the variables in the C language, but especially so for pointers. Lots of weird errors happen when a pointer isn't initialized.

We can't repeat it enough: Pointers must be initialized before they are used. The code below is similar to an example from an earlier chapter:

```
1       #include <stdio.h>
2
3       int main()
4       {
5               int pokey;
6
7               printf("The address of 'pokey' is
%p\n",&pokey);
8
9               return(0);
10      }
11
12
```

The ampersand operator fetches the address of the variable '*pokey*.'
The %p placeholder displays that address. Add an integer pointer
variable *p*. Remember, a pointer is a variable that holds a memory
address. To get that address, you use the ampersand operator.
That's already being used in this code, so you could figure this out
on your own. But just in case, we'll initialize the variable *p* for you at
line 8.

```
1       #include <stdio.h>
2
3       int main()
4       {
5               int pokey;
6               int *p;
7
```

```
8               p = &pokey;
9               printf("The address of 'pokey' is
%p\n",&pokey);
10
11              return(0);
12      }
13
14
```

The statement at line 8 assigns the address of variable *'pokey'* to the *p* pointer variable. At this point, you might be puzzled. You might say, "Where's the asterisk in front of the *p*?" We'll answer that question in a moment. But for now, remember that a pointer is a variable that holds a memory location. Here, that memory location is of the *'pokey'* variable.

Now, duplicate the *printf* statement. This time, replace *&pokey* with pointer variable *p*.

```
1       #include <stdio.h>
2
3       int main()
4       {
5               int pokey;
6               int *p;
7
8               p = &pokey;
9               printf("The address of 'pokey' is
%p\n",&pokey);
```

```
10              printf("The address of 'pokey' is %p\n",p);
11
12              return(0);
13      }
14
15
```

Save these changes and then build and run the code. As you can see, both lines output the same address. One is the address of variable *pokey* obtained with the ampersand. The other is the value saved in pointer variable *p*, which is that address.

DUAL NATURE OF POINTERS

While the pointer variable is declared by using an asterisk, it is not always used that way. Without the asterisk, the pointer variable represents a memory location. With the asterisk, the pointer represents the value at that location. This is the dual nature of the pointer variable. It is something that can be endlessly confusing. The code below is similar to the previous example, but we've initialized the '*pokey*' variable to the value 987:

```
1       #include <stdio.h>
2
3       int main()
4       {
5               int pokey;
6               int *p;
7
8               pokey = 987;
```

```
9              p = &pokey;

10

11             printf("The address of 'pokey' is
%p\n",&pokey);

12             printf("The contents of 'pokey' are
%d\n",pokey);

13

14             printf("The address of 'pokey' is %p\n",p);

15             printf("The contents of 'pokey' are
%d\n",*p);

16

17             return(0);

18     }

19

20
```

Two sets of *printf* statements display the address and value of the 'pokey' variable. The first set uses 'pokey' directly. The second set uses pointer variable *p*. In line 14, *p* is used without the asterisk, so it is a memory location. In line 15, *p* is used with the asterisk, so it peeks at the contents of that memory location. Build and run this code.

As you can see, the pointer variable *p* dutifully reports the correct values: the address and the contents. A logical question to ask at this point is, "Why bother?" At this level, using a pointer is pretty "pointless." You can do many things in C without bothering with pointers, but they do have their purpose. Many functions expect you to understand and know how pointers work.

ARRAY MANIPULATION USING POINTERS

Dealing with arrays is where pointers really come into play. After all, there is no such thing as an array in the C language. All arrays are simply shorthand for pointers. To prove it, in this section we dissect the common C language array. We'll show you how pointers can be used to manipulate an array, so as to provide flexibility and power other programming languages can only dream about.

```
1       #include <sdtio.h>
2
3       int main()
4       {
5               int array[] = { 11, 13, 17, 19 };
6               int x;
7
8               for(x=0;x<4;x++)
9               {
10                      printf("Element %d:
%d\n",x+1,array[x]);
11              }
12
13              return(0);
14      }
15
16
```

The code above is pretty basic. An array is declared, and its values assigned. A *for* loop marches through each element, displaying that element's value. Now take a look at the code below:

```
1       #include <stdio.h>
2
3       int main()
4         {
5               int array[] = { 11, 13, 17, 19 };
6               int x;
7               int *aptr;
8
9               aptr = array;          /*no & needed for an
array */
10
11              for(x=0;x<4;x++)
12                {
13                      printf("Element %d:
%d\n",x+1,*aptr);
14                              aptr++;
15                }
16
17              return(0);
18        }
19
20
```

This is pretty much the same code, but a pointer is used to display the array's values. The *aptr* variable is declared at line 7. It is initialized at line 9. An ampersand isn't needed here because arrays are all shorthand for pointers. The array name is really a memory location.

In the for loop, the *aptr* variable is used with the asterisk so that the value at the memory location is fetched. During the loop's first iteration, the value is the same as the 0th element in the array. Now, look at line 14. The *aptr* pointer variable is incremented.

In this format, the pointer variable is a memory location. The memory location is incremented. But by how much? Because *aptr* is an integer pointer, the memory address it holds is incremented by the size of an integer variable—the storage space that variable uses in memory. Conveniently, that happens to be the location of the next element in the array. Build and run the code.

As you can see, it works. The pointer variable is used to march through the array. The advantage here is that pointers can be used to manipulate array data. Pointers are variables. Take a look at the code below:

```
1       #include <sdtio.h>
2
3       int main()
4       {
5               int array[] = { 11, 13, 17, 19 };
6               int x;
7
8               for(x=0;x<4;x++)
9               {
10                      printf("Element %d:
%d\n",x+1,array[x]);
11              }
```

```
12
13              return(0);
14    }
15
16
```

Add a new line below line 6 to create a pointer variable, and then initialize the variable.

```
1       #include <sdtio.h>
2
3       int main()
4       {
5               int array[] = { 11, 13, 17, 19 };
6               int x;
7               int *aptr;
8
9               aptr = array;
10              for(x=0;x<4;x++)
11              {
12                      printf("Element %d: %d\n",x+1,array[x]);
13              }
14
15              return(0);
16    }
17
18
```

Set the value for the 3rd element to *zero* by using the pointer variable. The pointer variable is already referencing the first element in line 9. To reference the 3rd element, you need to add 2 to its value. To assign that memory location—the value *zero*—you use the asterisk operator.

```
1       #include <sdtio.h>
2
3       int main()
4       {
5               int array[] = { 11, 13, 17, 19 };
6               int x;
7               int *aptr;
8
9               aptr = array;
10              aptr = aptr + 2;
11              *aptr = 0;
12              for(x=0;x<4;x++)
13              {
14                      printf("Element %d: %d\n",x+1,array[x]);
15              }
16
17              return(0);
18      }
19
20
```

The rest of the code can remain the same. Save, build, and run the code. As you can see, the 3rd element is now *zero*. It has been manipulated by using a pointer.

Most C language programmers will combine the statements at line 10 and 11 into a single line. It looks like this:

```
1       #include <sdtio.h>

2

3       int main()

4       {

5               int array[] = { 11, 13, 17, 19 };

6               int x;

7               int *aptr;

8

9               aptr = array;

10              *(aptr+2) = 0;

11

12              for(x=0;x<4;x++)

13              {

14                      printf("Element %d: %d\n",x+1,array[x]);

15              }

16

17              return(0);

18      }

19

20
```

You need to use parenthesis because the pointer location must happen before the asterisk references the value. Save the changes, and then build and run the code. As you can see, the output is the same. You'll see this type of shorthand notation is used a lot. The main reason is that it doesn't affect the value of the *aptr* pointer variable, which still references the base address of the array.

Perhaps the best way to demonstrate pointer and array manipulation is to use strings, instead of numeric arrays. Take a look at the code below:

```
1       #include <stdio.h>
2
3       int main()
4       {
5               char *string = "I'm just a normal string.\n";
6
7               puts(string);
8
9               return(0);
10      }
11
12
```

In addition to declaring a string as a character array, you can also declare a string as a *char* pointer variable. The compiler makes the assignment, but the variable created is a pointer. In the code above, the variable pointer is used just like an array name here in the *puts* function. Build and run to confirm that this approach is not crazy.

Now, this begs the question that if you're afraid of pointers, how would you display this string one character at a time? Take a look at the code below:

```
1       #include <stdio.h>
2
3       int main()
4       {
5               char *string = "I'm just a normal string.\n";
6               int x = 0;
7
8               while(string[x])
9               {
10                      putchar(string[x]);
11                      x++;
12              }
13
14              return(0);
15      }
16
17
```

Yes, this is the "chicken" way to do it. It works because array notation is simply shorthand for pointers. In fact, many C programmers would do exactly as you see above, which is to use array notation to display the string. Build and run the code.

It works, but this approach is not why you're reading this book. We're going to replace the array notation with pointers. All you need is only one pointer, which we'll call '*ptr*,' and we don't need an *x*.

```
1      #include <stdio.h>
2
3      int main()
4      {
5              char *string = "I'm just a normal string.\n";
6              char *ptr;
7
8              ptr = string;
9              while(string[x])
10             {
11                     putchar(string[x]);
12                     x++;
13             }
14
15             return(0);
16     }
17
18
```

No ampersand is needed here because string is already a pointer—it holds a memory location. To examine a character at a memory location, the asterisk operator is used. The *while* loop's condition becomes ditto for the *putchar* function.

```
1      #include <stdio.h>
2
3      int main()
4      {
5              char *string = "I'm just a normal string.\n";
```

```
6            char *ptr;

7

8            ptr = string;

9            while(*ptr)

10           {

11                   putchar(*ptr);

12                   ptr++;

13           }

14

15           return(0);

16   }

17

18
```

Then you increment the memory location. Save the changes, and then build and run the code. As you can see, the output is still the same. Now you could go one step further if you like and not even use the 'ptr' variable. Let's make the necessary modifications in the code.

```
1        #include <stdio.h>

2

3        int main()

4        {

5                char *string = "I'm just a normal string.\n";

6

7

8

9                while(*string)
```

```
10              {
11                      putchar(*string);
12                      string++;
13              }
14
15              return(0);
16      }
17
18
```

Save, build and run the code. The issue here is that once you change the string variable, you lose its base location in memory. For this code, that is not an issue. But for other situations, it could present a problem.

POINTER FUNCTIONS

During your C programming lifetime, you'll often see pointers used whenever functions need or gives back pointer values. You'll be surprised how frequent this occurs in C programming. In this section, we will talk about how to address pointer functions, and even customize one. We will also discuss the many ways pointers are utilized in a function, how to transfer pointers to functions, and finally, how to give back pointers from functions.

There have been countless instances where we utilized functions in this book. You just probably did not recognize that it was happening. Take a look at the code below:

```
1      #include <stdio.h>

2

3      int main()

4      {

5              char x;

6

7              printf("Type a character: ");

8              scanf("%c",&x);

9              printf("Character %c\n",x);

10

11             return(0);

12     }

13

14
```

As you can see from the code above, the *scanf* function makes use of pointer values, particularly the variable it scans and their corresponding memory locations. At line 8 of the code, the ampersand symbol scans the memory location of variable x and passes it back to the function--*scanf*.

As you may have already noticed, the value that was returned to *scanf*--the return value--is not utilized in the function itself. What happens instead, is that the function makes use of a pointer to designate the value directly to variable x. Smart, isn't it?

In the code below, the ampersand symbol isn't needed for the variable *name*. Why? Well, the reason is because the variable *name* is basically an array.

```
1       #include <stdio.h>
2
3       int main()
4       {
5               char name[15];                  /* room for 14
characters */
6
7               printf("Your name? ");
8               scanf("%s",name);
9               printf("You are %s.\n",name);
10
11              return(0);
12      }
13
14
```

You can think of arrays as disguised pointers; the ampersand symbol is not required. You can customize your own C language function that uses a pointer. All you need to do is indicate a particular pointer as a return value, or as an argument. Note the code below:

```
1       #include <stdio.h>
2
3       void minus10(int *v);
4
5       int main()
6       {
7               int value = 100;
```

```
8
9              printf("Value is %d\n",value);
10             minus10(&value);
11             printf("Value is %d\n",value);
12
13             return(0);
14     }
15
16     void minus10(int *v)
17     {
18             *v = *v – 10;
19     }
20
21
```

As you can see in line 3 of the code above, the minus 10 function is prototyped. It also takes in an argument: a pointer variable. The pointer variable is basically a memory address, so the function basically accepts a memory address as an argument. The variable value's memory location/address is then transferred to the function, which you can see at line 10. As usual, the ampersand symbol fetches that address.

Within the function, the value of the transferred variable is changed using the asterisk. Since the variable's values are straightaway scanned in memory, no returned value is required. Build and run this code.

As you can see, the function has a direct impact on the value of the variable. This is true even though the only thing that was transferred to the function was the memory address and there was no return value. Now look at the code below:

```
1       #include <stdio.h>
2       #include <string.h>
3
4       char *longer(char *s1, char *s2);
5
6       int main()
7       {
8               char *string1 = "A long time ago";
9               char *string2 = "In a galaxy far, far away";
10              char *result;
11
12              result = longer(string1,string2);
13              printf("String '%s' is longer.\n",result);
14
15              return(0);
16      }
17
18      char *longer(char *s1, char *s2)
19      {
20              int len1,len2;
21
22          len1 = strlen(s1);
23          len2 = strlen(s2);
24
25              if( len 1 > len 2 )
```

```
26                    return(s1);
27          else
28                    return(s2);
29     }
30
31
```

In the code above, you can see that a pointer function is declared. *Longer* basically gives back the memory address of the beginning of a string stored in memory—the character pointer. The function that starts from line 18 onwards makes a comparison of the two strings. Specifically, it uses the string's length for comparison. What's returned is the memory address of the string that has the longest length.

Note that the string itself is not the one that makes its way back to the function. The one that makes it back is the string's memory location/address. That address is then stored within the pointer *result*, which is then displayed at line 13. Build and run this code. As you can see, what's displayed is the longest string.

You also may be able to manipulate strings within functions. As what we've stated before, you are not passing any string per se. You are basically only passing its starting memory location/address in memory. Look at the code below:

```
1     #include <stdio.h>
2     #include <ctype.h>
3
```

```
4       void shouting(char *input);

5

6    int main()

7    {

8            char string[64];

9

10           printf("Type some text: ");

11           fgets(string,64,stdin);

12           printf("You typed:\n%s\n",string);

13           shouting(string);

14           printf("If you were shouting, you'd
typed:\n%s\n",string);

15

16           return(0);

17   }

18

19   void shouting(char *input)

20   {

21           while(*input)

22           {

23                   *input = toupper(*input);

24                   input++;

25           }

26   }

27

28
```

The code above is one example of making use of pointers to manipulate a string in a function, where the function is not required to give any value back. At line 19, the function 'shouting' receives a string and chews through it one character after another. Each and every character scanned is then sent to the toupper function.

The toupper function, if you still remember from our discussions in the previous chapters, converts any lowercase letter to uppercase, hence the name 'toupper.' Build and run this code. As you can see, the program works like a charm. It works all without the need to return any value from the function. Now look at the code below:

```
1       #include <stdio.h>
2       #include <ctype.h>
3
4       char *encrypt(char *input);
5
6       int main()
7       {
8               char *instructions = "Deliver the package to
Berlin";
9
10              printf("Here are your secret
instructions:\n%s\n",encrypt(instructions));
11
12              return(0);
13      }
14
15      char *encrypt(char *input)
16      {
17              char output[64];
```

```
18              int x = 0;
19
20              while(*input)
21              {
22                      if(isalpha(*input))
23                              output[x] = *input + 1;
24                      else
25                              output[x] = *input;
26                      x++;
27                      input++;
28              }
29      }
30
31
```

In the sample code shown above, the encrypt function returns a string. An array of characters--a string--is received by the function, manipulated, then a new string is given back, all the while keeping the original string unchanged. Will this work? Let's take a look. Build and run this code.

It is likely that you'll see a compiler warning after running the code. It is a serious warning that gives an explanation as to why the output of the code is dubious. Contrary to what you might be thinking, pointers are not the culprit here. What's happening is basically an old instance we discussed in a previous chapter about functions, which is all variables are considered 'local' when used within functions.

Once the execution of the function is over, all the variables utilized are discarded. This is the same for the function *'encrypt'* with the array *'output.'*

To remedy this problem, what you need to do is make use of the keyword *static*. In line 17 of the code, insert the *static* keyword at the beginning of the variable declaration.

```
1       #include <stdio.h>
2       #include <ctype.h>
3
4       char *encrypt(char *input);
5
6       int main()
7       {
8               char *instructions = "Deliver the package to
Berlin";
9
10              printf("Here are your secret
instructions:\n%s\n",encrypt(instructions));
11
12              return(0);
13      }
14
15      char *encrypt(char *input)
16      {
17              static char output[64];
18              int x = 0;
19
```

```
20              while(*input)
21              {
22                      if(isalpha(*input))
23                              output[x] = *input + 1;
24              else
25                              output[x] = *input;
26                      x++;
27                      input++;
28              }
29      }
30
31
```

With the *static* keyword in place, the program is now able to retain the array's content when the function finishes its execution. The function remains static. In other words, it remains unchanged. Save, build and run this code. The *encrypt* function only returns the memory address/location of the string. The other characters still reside in memory and are referenced by the *printf* function. Remember that all of this will only work if you ensure that the returned string is *static*.

Do note, however, that this particular rule isn't applicable to single values. C language functions are designed to give back single values, which also includes pointers. For other arrays, strings, or any kind of variable within a function, you have to make sure that they are static. Or else the value isn't retained as soon as the function finishes executing.

POINTER ARRAYS

Just like what we mentioned previously, pointers are variables. It is a specific type of variable that stores a particular memory location. Being a variable, it is also possible to set pointers inside arrays--a thought that's very frightening to some. This section's main topic is how and why to put pointers inside an array. Here, we'll discuss how to setup a pointer array in the C language.

For the sake of simplicity, we'll utilize strings for our example. You'll learn how to retrieve strings, transform them from one notation to another, and how to evaluate strings. Pointer arrays are basically a stockpile of memory locations. When and why would you require an array—a stockpile—of memory locations? Well, one exemplary example is to make use of a string array.

Take a look at the code below:

```
1       #include <stdio.h>
2
3       int main()
4       {
5               char *gang[5] = {
6                       "Spanky",
7                       "Buckwheat",
8                       "Alfalfa",
9                       "Darla",
10                      "Pete the Pup"
11              };
12              int x;
```

```
13
14              for(x=0;x<5;x++)
15                  printf("%s\n",gang[x]);
16
17              return(0);
18      }
19
20
```

The code creates room for exactly five memory addresses/locations. These addresses are predefined to the listed strings. As a matter of fact, a string array is declared, although technically it is not correct. The strings are then sent to standard output with the use of a *for* loop, which you can see at line 14 of the code. Build and run the code.

As you can clearly see from the output, each of the five strings is displayed. To prove that the array is a clutch of memory locations, modify the code. In line 15, change the %s placeholder to %p. Remember that %p is the memory location or address placeholder.

```
1       #include <stdio.h>
2
3       int main()
4       {
5               char *gang[5] = {
6                   "Spanky",
7                   "Buckwheat",
8                   "Alfalfa",
```

```
9                    "Darla",
10                   "Pete the Pup"
11           };
12           int x;
13
14           for(x=0;x<5;x++)
15                   printf("%p\n",gang[x]);
16
17           return(0);
18     }
19
20
```

Save the change, and then build and run the code. Now you see a series of memory locations. Because the compiler allocated space for the strings and stuck null characters at the end, each memory location does reference a string. By the way, this method of storing multiple strings is far more efficient than declaring a two-dimensional array.

In that case, you must declare the array so that each string occupies as many characters of storage as the longest string. At our code's pointer array declaration, that's not an issue. Take a look at the code below:

```
1      #include <stdio.h>
2
3      int main()
4        {
```

```
5                    char *gang[5] = {
6                            "Spanky",
7                            "Buckwheat",
8                            "Alfalfa",
9                            "Darla",
10                           "Pete the Pup"
11                   };
12                   int x;
13                   char *cptr;
14
15                   for(x=0;x<5;x++)
16                   {
17                           cptr = gang[x];
18                           while(*cptr)
19                           {
20                                   putchar(*cptr);
21                                   cptr++;
22                           }
23                           putchar('\n');
24                   }
25
26                   return(0);
27           }
28
29
```

This code is another version of the previous example. Here, the for loop moves through each pointer in the array. For each iteration, the pointer variable cptr is assigned to the base address of each string. A *while* loop then churns through the strings one character at a time. Build and run this code.

The output is the same, although the method of printing each string was different. Pointer variable *cptr* is used to display each character by walking through the memory locations where the characters are stored. Now something might bother you about this code. That's line 17, if you haven't picked it up already. It uses array notation.

A better solution would be to convert this heinous notation into pointer notation. To do so, make this change to the code:

```
1      #include <stdio.h>
2
3      int main()
4      {
5              char *gang[5] = {
6                      "Spanky",
7                      "Buckwheat",
8                      "Alfalfa",
9                      "Darla",
10                     "Pete the Pup"
11             };
12             int x;
13             char *cptr;
14
15             for(x=0;x<5;x++)
16             {
17                     cptr = *(gang+x);
```

```
18                      while(*cptr)
19                      {
20                              putchar(*cptr);
21                              cptr++;
22                      }
23                      putchar('\n');
24              }
25
26              return(0);
27      }
28
29
```

This notation uses the memory addresses stored in the *gang* variable. The memory locations are used, not the string. Then the value *x* is added to each, and each time the loop references the next array element, which is the base address of a string. It has to be enclosed in parenthesis because the memory location is manipulated first. Then the contents of that location—the asterisk fetches the string—is referenced later. Save the changes, and then build and run the code.

As you can see, the output is the same. More can be done with pointers here, and we could broach upon the topic of pointers to pointers and all double asterisk notation. But that's more of a topic for an advanced level. In fact, here's a tip: When you see the dreaded double asterisk pointer notation, it is almost always a sign that you're dealing with an array of strings, or specifically, an array of memory locations for each of those strings.

CONCLUSION

There you have it. That is all there is to the basics of C programming. The only reason all of this is scary, and the only reason anybody is nervous about programming in C, is because they do not have a firm foundation of the basics of the C programming language. Once you understand the basic syntax and various elements of C, it all gets exceptionally easy.

The topics covered in this book, though they might seem complicated to you at this point, is just pretty basic. We are confident that everything that we've covered in this book will help you get a firm grasp of the basics of C. In addition, this book will help you fully understand the more advanced levels of C language, such as object oriented C programming.

We would like to thank you for buying this book. We hope that you learned a lot about the C programming language. Feel free to make this book your beginner's quick guide as you explore the intricacies of this fantastic programming language.

At this point, we would like to encourage you to tinker and play around with the C programming language. Try making programs of your own and see where it leads you.

The C language is truly an amazing programming language. We hope that this book becomes your stepping stone into being a well-rounded programmer.